FOR YOUR DELIGHT

Wilfred Pickles

FOR YOUR DELIGHT

A personal selection of
poetry for all occasions

W. H. ALLEN
LONDON
1960

I dedicate this book to you who love good poetry. I hope the poems I have chosen will bring you as much delight as they have always brought me.

Wilfred Pickles

Made and printed in Great Britain by
Cox & Wyman Ltd., London, Fakenham and Reading, for the
publishers W. H. Allen & Co. Ltd., Essex Street, London, W.C.2

ACKNOWLEDGMENTS

My thanks are due to all the people who have kindly allowed me to include their poems in this anthology, including Mr. R. F. Delderfield, Miss Violet Jacob, Miss Jill Jellicoe, Mr. T. Lovatt Williams and Mr. Louis MacNeice.

Also to

Mrs. John Drinkwater and Messrs. Samuel French Ltd., for *At Grafton* by John Drinkwater.

Mr. Siegfried Sassoon, for *The Dreamers*.

Mrs. Harold Monro, for *Milk for the Cat* by Harold Monro.

Miss Joan Townsend, for *Lookin' Back*.

Mrs. Miller, for *Pendle Nestlin' Song*.

Mrs. Cornford, for *Autumn Evening*.

Messrs. Wm. Heinemann & Co. Ltd., for *The Turkish Trench Dog* by Geoffrey Dearmer, from *Poems*.

Miss Joan Sparks, for *Roundabouts and Swings* by Patrick R. Chalmers.

The Society of Authors, Dr. John Masefield, O.M. and The Macmillan Company, New York, for *Laugh and be merry*, *The West Wind*, *Sea Fever* and *Cargoes*.

The Society of Authors as the literary representatives of the Trustees of the Estate of the late A. E. Housman, and Messrs. Jonathan Cape Ltd., publishers of A. E. Housman's *Collected Poems*, for *The Chestnut Casts His Flambeaux* by A. E. Housman.

The Executors of the late Dr. Alfred Noyes, for *The Highwayman*.

Mr. Ralph Hodgson and Messrs. Macmillan & Co. Ltd., for *Time, You Old Gipsy Man* and *The Bells of Heaven* from *Poems*.

Lady Salmond, for *Into Battle* by Julian Grenfell.

Mr. W. H. Auden, for *Oh the Valley in the Summer*.

Mr. Wilfrid Gibson and Messrs. Macmillan & Co. Ltd., for *Lament*.

Messrs. Frederick Muller Ltd., for *Lost in France* by Ernest Rhys.

Mr. Michael Ayrton, for *I am Frightened, Sweetheart* and *The Silver Mist along the the River Dims* by Gerald Gould.

Mr. John Betjeman and Messrs. John Murray (Publishers) Ltd., for *A Subaltern's Love-Song* and *Indoor Games Near Newbury* from *Collected Poems of John Betjeman*.

Messrs. John Murray (Publishers) Ltd., for *Tim, an Irish Terrier* by Winifred Mary Letts, *Tam i' the Kirk* by Violet Jacob and *Before Action* by William Noel Hodgson.

Messrs. The Bodley Head Ltd., for *My Will* from *Selected Poems of Arthur Benson* and *My Old Friend* from *Lord Vyet* by Arthur Benson.

Messrs. Sidgwick & Jackson Ltd. and Messrs. McClelland & Stewart Ltd., for *The Soldier* and *The Old Vicarage, Granchester* from *The Collected Poems of Rupert Brooke*.

Mr. A. E. O'Gioballain, for *The Third Adam*.

Mr. John Pudney and Messrs. Putnam & Co. Ltd., for *Aunts watching Television* and *20th Valediction*.

Messrs. J. M. Dent & Sons Ltd., for *To a Poet a Thousand Years Hence* by James Elroy Flecker.

Mrs. George Bambridge and the Macmillan Company of Canada, for *Chant-Pagan* by Rudyard Kipling.

Miss D. E. Collins and Messrs. Methuen & Co. Ltd., for *The Rolling English Road* from *The Flying Inn*, and *The Donkey* from *The Wild Knight* by G. K. Chesterton.

Captain Francis Newbolt, C.M.G. and Messrs. John Murray (Publishers) Ltd., for *Vitai Lampada* from *Poems Old & New*.

Dorothy Una Ratcliffe, the Yorkshire Dialect Society and Messrs. Nelson & Sons Ltd., for *Yorkshire Five*.

Messrs. Cobden Sanderson Ltd., for *The Child's Grave* and *Forefathers* from *Collected Poems of Edmund Blunden*.

Messrs. MacDonald & Co. Ltd., for *Jim* and *Matilda* from *Cautionary Tales* and *The South Country* from *Sonnets and Verse* by Hilaire Belloc.

Messrs. Secker & Warburg, for *Miss Thompson Goes Shopping* by Martin Armstrong.

CONTENTS

DEATH

FOR CHILDREN AND ABOUT CHILDREN

[9]

LIFE

'SOLDIERS'

OLD FAVOURITES

To a Poet a Thousand Years Hence

I who am dead a thousand years,
    And wrote this sweet archaic song,
Send you my words for messengers
    The way I shall not pass along.

I care not if you bridge the seas,
    Or ride secure the cruel sky,
Or build consummate palaces
    Of metal or of masonry.

But have you wine and music still,
    And statues and a bright-eyed love,
And foolish thoughts of good or ill,
    And prayers to them who sit above?

How shall we conquer? Like a wind
    That falls at eve our fancies blow,
And old Maeonides the blind
    Said it three thousand years ago.

O friend unseen, unborn, unknown,
    Student of our sweet English tongue,
Read out my words at night, alone,
    I was a poet, I was young.

Since I can never see your face,
    And never shake you by the hand,
I send my soul through time and space
    To greet you. You will understand.

                    JAMES ELROY FLECKER 1884–1915

LOVE

To an Inconstant One

I loved thee once; I'll love no more—
  Thine be the grief as is the blame;
Thou art not what thou wast before,
    What reason I should be the same?
      He that can love unloved again,
      Hath better store of love than brain:
      God send me love my debts to pay,
      While unthrifts fool their love away!

Nothing could have my love o'erthrown
  If thou hadst still continued mine;
Yea, if thou hadst remain'd thy own,
    I might perchance have yet been thine.
      But thou thy freedom didst recall
      That it thou might elsewhere enthrall
      And then how could I but disdain
      A captive's captive to remain?

When new desires had conquer'd thee
  And changed the object of thy will,
It had been lethargy in me,
    Not constancy, to love thee still.
      Yea, it had been a sin to go
      And prostitute affection so:
      Since we are taught no prayers to say
      To such as must to others pray.

Yet do thou glory in thy choice—
  Thy choice of his good fortune boast;
I'll neither grieve nor yet rejoice
    To see him gain what I have lost:
      The height of my disdain shall be
      To laugh at him, to blush for thee;
      To love thee still, but go no more
      A-begging at a beggar's door.

SIR ROBERT AYTON 1847–1922

Renouncement

I must not think of thee; and, tired yet strong,
    I shun the love that lurks in all delight—
  The love of thee—and in the blue heaven's height,
And in the dearest passage of a song.
Oh, just beyond the sweetest thoughts that throng
    This breast, the thought of thee waits hidden yet
        bright;
    But it must never, never come in sight;
I must stop short of thee the whole day long.
But when sleep comes to close each difficult day,
    When night gives pause to the long watch I keep,
And all my bonds I needs must loose apart,
Must doff my will as raiment laid away,—
    With the first dream that comes with the first sleep,
I run, I run, I am gathered to thy heart.

ALICE MEYNELL

Edith and Harold

I know it will not ease the smart;
    I know it will increase the pain;
'Tis torture to a wounded heart;
    Yet, O! to see him once again.

Tho' other lips be press'd to his,
    And other arms about him twine,
And tho' another reign in bliss
    In that true heart that once was mine;

Yet, O! I cry it in my grief,
    I cry it blindly in my pain,
I know it will not bring relief,
    Yet O! to see him once again.

ARTHUR GRAY BUTLER

Oh the Valley in the Summer where I and My John

Oh the valley in the summer where I and my John
Beside the deep river would walk on and on
While the flowers at our feet and the birds up above
Argued so sweetly on reciprocal love,
And I leaned on his shoulder; 'O Johnny, let's play':
But he frowned like thunder and he went away.

O that Friday near Christmas as I well recall
When we went to the Charity Matinee Ball,
The floor was so smooth and the band was so loud
And Johnny so handsome I felt so proud;
'Squeeze me tighter, dear Johnny, let's dance till it's day:
But he frowned like thunder and he went away.

Shall I ever forget at the Grand Opera
When music poured out of each wonderful star?
Diamonds and pearls they hung dazzling down
Over each silver or golden silk gown;
'O John I'm in heaven', I whispered to say:
But he frowned like thunder and he went away.

O but he was as fair as a garden in flower,
As slender and tall as the great Eiffel Tower,
When the waltz throbbed out on the long promenade
O his eyes and his smile they went straight to my heart;
'O marry me, Johnny, I'll love and obey':
But he frowned like thunder and he went away.

O last night I dreamed of you, Johnny, my lover,
You'd the sun on one arm and the moon on the other,
The sea it was blue and the grass it was green,
Every star rattled a round tambourine;
Ten thousand miles deep in a pit where I lay:
But you frowned like thunder and you went away.

W. H. AUDEN

[19]

Youth and Art

It once might have been once only:
We lodged in a street together,
You, a sparrow on the housetop lonely,
I, a lone she-bird of his feather.

Your trade was with sticks and clay,
You thumbed, thrust, patted and polished,
Then laughed 'They will see some day
'Smith made, and Gibson demolished.'

My business was song, song, song;
I chirped, cheeped, trilled and twittered,
'Kate Brown's on the boards ere long,
'And Grisi's existence embittered!'

I earned no more by a warble
Than you by a sketch in plaster;
You wanted a piece of marble,
I needed a music-master.

We studied hard in our styles,
Chipped each at a crust like Hindoos,
For air looked out on the tiles,
For fun watched each other's windows.

You lounged, like a boy of the South,
Cap and blouse—nay, a bit of beard too;
Or you got it, rubbing your mouth
With fingers the clay adhered to.

And I—soon managed to find
Weak points in the flower-fence facing,
Was forced to put up a blind
And be safe in my corset-lacing.

No harm! It was not my fault
If you never turned your eye's tail up

As I shook upon E in alt,
Or ran the chromatic scale up:

For spring bade the sparrows pair,
And the boys and girls gave guesses,
And stalls in our street looked rare
With bulrush and watercresses.

Why did not you pinch a flower
In a pellet of clay and fling it?
Why did not I put a power
Of thanks in a look, or sing it?

I did look, sharp as a lynx,
(And yet the memory rankles)
When models arrived, some minx
Tripped up-stairs, she and her ankles.

But I think I gave you as good!
'That foreign fellow,—who can know
'How she pays, in a playful mood,
'For his tuning her that piano?'

Could you say so, and never say
'Suppose we join hands and fortunes,
'And I fetch her from over the way,
'Her, piano, and long tunes and short tunes?'

No, no: you would not be rash,
Nor I rasher and something over:
You've to settle yet Gibson's hash,
And Grisi yet lives in clover.

But you meet the Prince at the Board,
I'm queen myself at bals-pare,
I've married a rich old lord,
And you're dubbed knight and an R.A.

Each life unfulfilled, you see;
It hangs still, patchy and scrappy:

[21]

We have not sighed deep, laughed free,
Starved, feasted, despaired—been happy.

And nobody calls you a dunce,
And people suppose me clever:
This could but have happened once,
And we missed it, lost it for ever.

ROBERT BROWNING. 1812–1889

False Though She Be

False though she be to me and love,
    I'll ne'er pursue revenge;
For still the charmer I approve,
    Though I deplore her change.

In hours of bliss we oft have met:
    They could not always last;
And though the present I regret,
    I'm grateful for the past.

WILLIAM CONGREVE. 1670–1729

Why so Pale and Wan, Fond Lover

Why so pale and wan, fond lover?
    Prithee why so pale?
Will, when looking well can't move her,
    Looking ill prevail?
    Prithee why so pale?

Why so dull and mute, young sinner?
    Prithee why so mute?
Will, when speaking well can't win her,
    Saying nothing do't?
    Prithee why so mute?

Quit, quit for shame, this will not move,

[22]

This cannot take her;
If of her self she will not love,
Nothing can make her.
The divel take her!

SIR JOHN SUCKLING. 1609–1642

Shadows

They seem'd, to those who saw them meet,
The casual friends of every day;
Her smile was undisturb'd and sweet,
His courtesy was free and gay.

But yet if one the other's name
In some unguarded moment heard,
The heart you thought so calm and tame
Would struggle like a captured bird:

And letters of mere formal phrase
Were blister'd with repeated tears,—
And this was not the work of days,
But had gone on for years and years!

RICHARD MONCKTON MILNES, LORD HOUGHTON. 1809–1885

A Subaltern's Love-Song

Miss J. Hunter Dunn, Miss J. Hunter Dunn,
Furnish'd and burnish'd by Aldershot sun,
What strenuous singles we played after tea,
We in the tournament—you against me!

Love-thirty, love-forty, oh! weakness of joy,
The speed of a swallow, the grace of a boy,
With carefullest carelessness, gaily you won,
I am weak from your loveliness, Joan Hunter Dunn.

Miss Joan Hunter Dunn, Miss Joan Hunter Dunn,

[23]

How mad I am, sad I am, glad that you won.
The warm-handled racket is back in its press,
But my shock-headed victor, she loves me no less.

Her father's euonymus shines as we walk,
And swing past the summer-house, buried in talk,
And cool the verandah that welcomes us in
To the six-o'clock news and a lime-juice and gin.

The scent of the conifers, sound of the bath,
The view from my bedroom of moss-dappled path,
As I struggle with double-end evening tie,
For we dance at the Golf Club, my victor and I.

On the floor of her bedroom lie blazer and shorts
And the cream-coloured walls are be-trophied with sports,
And westering, questioning settles the sun
On your low-leaded window, Miss Joan Hunter Dunn.

The Hillman is waiting, the light's in the hall,
The pictures of Egypt are bright on the wall,
My sweet, I am standing beside the oak stair
And there on the landing's the light on your hair.

By roads 'not adopted', by woodlanded ways,
She drove to the club in the late summer haze,
Into nine-o'clock Camberley, heavy with bells
And mushroomy, pine-woody, evergreen smells.

Miss Joan Hunter Dunn, Miss Joan Hunter Dunn,
I can hear from the car-park the dance has begun.
Oh! full Surrey twilight! importunate band!
Oh! strongly adorable tennis-girl's hand!

Around us are Rovers and Austins afar,
Above us, the intimate roof of the car,
And here on my right is the girl of my choice,
With the tilt of her nose and the chime of her voice,

And the scent of her wrap, and the words never said,

And the ominous, ominous dancing ahead.
We sat in the car park till twenty to one
And now I'm engaged to Miss Joan Hunter Dunn.

JOHN BETJEMAN

To a Young Lady

Polly, from me, tho' now a love-sick youth,
    Nay, tho' a poet, hear the voice of truth!
Polly, you're not a beauty, yet you're pretty;
So grave, yet gay; so silly, yet so witty;
A heart of softness, yet a tongue of satire;
You've cruelty, yet, ev'n in that, good-nature:
Now you are free, and now reserv'd a while;
Now a forc'd frown betrays a willing smile.
Reproach'd for absence, yet your sight deny'd;
My tongue you silence, yet my silence chide.
How wou'd you praise me, shou'd your sex defame!
Yet, shou'd they praise, grow jealous, and exclaim.
If I despair, with some kind look you bless;
But if I hope, at once all hope suppress.
You scorn; yet shou'd my passion change or fail,
Too late you'd whimper out a softer tale.
You love; yet from your lover's wish retire;
Doubt, yet discern; deny, and yet desire,
Such, Polly, are your sex—part truth, part fiction,
Some thought, much whim, and all a contradiction.

RICHARD SAVAGE. 1698–1743

I am Frightened Sweetheart—

I am frightened, sweetheart—that's the long and short
    Of the bad mind I bear: the scent comes back
    Of an unhappy garden gone to wrack,
The flower-beds trampled for an idiot's sport,
A mass of vermin batt'ning there, a mort
    Of weeds a-fester, all the green turned black,

[25]

And through the sodden glades of loss and lack
The dead winds blow of hate and false report.

There was a music in the early air,
When our young love was virgin as we were,
    Ripe for the rose, new to the nightingale;
But now two ghosts walk showing each to each
The empty grace of ceremonious speech,
    And I am frightened, and the air is stale.

GERALD GOULD

The Silver Mist Along the River Dims

The silver mist along the river dims
    The middle landscape and the distant hills;
    It waxes imperceptibly, and fills
The evening with a sense of dreams and whims,
And great Orion of the starry limbs
    Is blotted out, and melancholy kills
    Earth's wandering hopes with its insistent chills,
And the late birds forget their twilight hymns.

The mist clings in your eyebrows and your hair—
    The silver starry web, the net of tears;
Your slim and startled body, unaware,
    Clings in my arms for warmth; a thousand fears
Torment the cloudy texture of the air,
    As, bit by bit, our known world disappears.

GERALD GOULD

Eileen Aroon

When like the early rose,
        Eileen Aroon!
Beauty in childhood blows,
        Eileen Aroon!

[26]

When, like a diadem,
Buds blush around the stem,
Which is the fairest gem?—
   Eileen Aroon!

Is it the laughing eye,
   Eileen Aroon!
Is it the timid sigh,
   Eileen Aroon!
Is it the tender tone,
Soft as the string'd harp's moan?
O, it is truth alone,—
   Eileen Aroon!

When like the rising day,
   Eileen Aroon!
Love sends his early ray,
   Eileen Aroon!
What makes his dawning glow,
Changeless through joy or woe?
Only the constant know:—
   Eileen Aroon!

I knew a valley fair,
   Eileen Aroon!
I knew a cottage there,
   Eileen Aroon!
Far in that valley's shade
I knew a gentle maid,
Flower of a hazel glade,—
   Eileen Aroon!

Who in the song so sweet?
   Eileen Aroon!
Who in the dance so fleet?
   Eileen Aroon!
Dear were her charms to me,
Dearer her laughter free,
Dearest her constancy,—
   Eileen Aroon.

Were she no longer true,
                Eileen Aroon!
What should her lover do?
                Eileen Aroon!
Fly with his broken chain
Far o'er the sounding main,
Never to love again,—
                Eileen Aroon!

Youth most with time decay,
                Eileen Aroon!
Beauty must fade away,
                Eileen Aroon!
Castles are sack'd in war,
Chieftains are scatter'd far
Truth is a fixed star,—
                Eileen Aroon.

GERALD GRIFFIN. 1803–1840

At Her Window

Beating Heart! we come again
        Where my Love reposes:
This is Mabel's window-pane;
        These are Mabel's roses.

Is she nested? Does she kneel
        In the twilight stilly,
Lily clad from throat to heel,
        She, my virgin Lily?

Soon the wan, the wistful stars,
        Fading, will forsake her;
Elves of light, on beamy bars,
        Whisper then, and wake her.

Let this friendly pebble plead
        At her flowery grating;

If she hear me will she heed?
　　Mabel, I am waiting!

Mabel will be deck'd anon,
　　Zoned in bride's apparel;
Happy zone! O hark to yon
　　Passion-shaken carol!

Sing thy song, thou tranced thrush,
　　Pipe thy best, thy clearest;—
Hush, her lattice moves, O hush—
　　Dearest Mabel!—dearest . . .

FREDERICK LOCKER-LAMPSON

To the Virgins, to Make Much of Time

Gather ye rosebuds while ye may,
　　Old Time is still a-flying:
And this same flower that smiles to-day
　　To-morrow will be dying.

The glorious lamp of heaven, the sun,
　　The higher he's a-getting,
The sooner will his race be run,
　　And nearer he's to setting.

That age is best which is the first,
　　When youth and blood are warmer;
But being spent, the worse, and worst
　　Times still succeed the former.

Then be not coy, but use your time,
　　And while ye may, go marry:
For having lost but once your prime,
　　You may for ever tarry.

ROBERT HERRICK. 1591–1674

To Anthea, Who May Command Him Anything

Bid me to live, and I will live
  Thy Protestant to be;
Or bid me love, and I will give
  A loving heart to thee.

A heart as soft, a heart as kind,
  A heart as sound and free
As in the whole world thou canst find,
  That heart I'll give to thee.

Bid that heart stay, and it will stay
  To honour thy decree:
Or bid it languish quite away,
  And't shall do so for thee.

Bid me to weep, and I will weep
  While I have eyes to see:
And, having none, yet I will keep
  A heart to weep for thee.

Bid me despair, and I'll despair
  Under that cypress-tree:
Or bid me die, and I will dare
  E'en death to die for thee.

Thou art my life, my love, my heart,
  The very eyes of me:
And hast command of every part
  To live and die for thee.

ROBERT HERRICK. 1591–1674

On a Girdle

That which her slender waist confined
  Shall now my joyful temples bind;

[30]

No monarch but would give his crown
His arms might do what this has done.

It was my Heaven's extremest sphere,
The pale which held that lovely deer:
My joy, my grief, my hope, my love,
Did all within this circle move.

A narrow compass! and yet there
Dwelt all that's good, and all that's fair!
Give me but what this ribband bound,
Take all the rest the sun goes round!

EDMUND WALLER. 1606–1687

Memory

So shuts the marigold her leaves
    At the departure of the sun;
So from the honeysuckle sheaves
    The bee goes when the day is done;
So sits the turtle when she is but one,
And so all woe, as I since she is gone.

To some few birds kind Nature hath
    Made all the summer as one day:
Which once enjoy'd, cold winter's wrath
    As night they sleeping pass away.
Those happy creatures are, that know not yet
The pain to be deprived or to forget.

I oft have heard men say there be
    Some that with confidence profess
The helpful Art of Memory:
    But could they teach Forgetfulness,
I'd learn; and try what further art could do
To make me love her and forget her too.

WILLIAM BROWNE. 1590–1645

[31]

The Bargain

My true love hath my heart, and I have his,
    By just exchange one for another given:
I hold his dear, and mine he cannot miss,
    There never was a better bargain driven:
        My true love hath my heart, and I have his.

His heart in me keeps him and me in one,
    My heart in him his thoughts and senses guides:
He loves my heart, for once it was his own,
    I cherish his because in me it bides:
        My true love hath my heart, and I have his.

SIR PHILIP SIDNEY. 1554–1586

To His Coy Love

I pray thee, leave, love me no more,
    Call home the heart you gave me!
I but in vain that saint adore
    That can but will not save me.
These poor half-kisses kill me quite—
    Was ever man thus served?
Amidst an ocean of delight
    For pleasure to be starved?

Show me no more those snowy breasts
    With azure riverets branched,
Where, whilst mine eye with plenty feasts,
    Yet is my thirst not stanched;
O Tantalus, thy pains ne'er tell!
    By me thou art prevented:
'Tis nothing to be plagued in Hell,
    But thus in Heaven tormented.

Clip me no more in those dear arms,
    Nor thy life's comfort call me,

O these are but too powerful charms,
　　And do but more enthral me!
But see how patient I am grown
　　In all this coil about thee:
Come, nice thing, let my heart alone,
　　I cannot live without thee!

MICHAEL DRAYTON. 1563–1631

Sweet-and-Twenty

O mistress mine, where are you roaming?
　　O, stay and hear! your true love's coming,
That can sing both high and low:
Trip no further, pretty sweeting;
Journeys end in lovers meeting,
　　Every wise man's son doth know.

What is love? 'tis not hereafter;
Present mirth hath present laughter;
　　What's to come is still unsure:
In delay there lies no plenty;
Then come kiss me, sweet-and-twenty!
　　Youth's a stuff will not endure.

WILLIAM SHAKESPEARE. 1564–1616

Sonnet

When, in disgrace with Fortune and men's eyes,
　　I all alone beweep my outcast state,
And trouble deaf heaven with my bootless cries,
And look upon myself, and curse my fate,
Wishing me like to one more rich in hope,
Featured like him, like him with friends possest,
Desiring this man's art and that man's scope,
With what I most enjoy contented least;
Yet in these thoughts myself almost despising—
Haply I think on thee: and then my state,

C
[33]

Like to the Lark at break of day arising
From sullen earth, sings hymns at Heaven's gate;
        For thy sweet love rememb'red such wealth brings
        That then I scorn to change my state with Kings.

WILLIAM SHAKESPEARE. 1564–1616

Sonnet

Being your slave, what should I do but tend
        Upon the hours and times of your desire?
I have no precious time at all to spend,
Nor services to do, till you require.
Nor dare I chide the world-without-end hour
Whilst I, my sovereign, watch the clock for you,
Nor think the bitterness of absence sour
When you have bid your servant once adieu;
Nor dare I question with my jealous thought
Where you may be, or your affairs suppose,
But, like a sad slave, stay and think of nought
Save, where you are how happy you make those!
        So true a fool is love, that in your Will,
        Though you do any thing, he thinks no ill.

WILLIAM SHAKESPEARE. 1564–1616

Hidden Flame

I feed a flame within, which so torments me
        That it both pains my heart, and yet contents me:
'Tis such a pleasing smart, and I so love it,
That I had rather die than once remove it.

Yet he, for whom I grieve, shall never know it;
My tongue does not betray, nor my eyes show it.
Not a sigh, nor a tear, my pain discloses,
But they fall silently, like dew on roses.

Thus, to prevent my Love from being cruel,

[34]

My heart's the sacrifice, as 'tis the fuel;
And while I suffer this to give him quiet,
My faith rewards my love, though he deny it.

On his eyes will I gaze, and there delight me;
While I conceal my love no frown can fright me.
To be more happy I dare not aspire,
Nor can I fall more low, mounting no higher.

JOHN DRYDEN. 1631–1700

The Reconcilement

Come, let us now resolve at last
    To live and love in quiet;
We'll tie the knot so very fast
    That Time shall ne'er untie it.

The truest joys they seldom prove
    Who free from quarrels live:
'Tis the most tender part of love
    Each other to forgive.

When least I seem'd concern'd, I took
    No pleasure nor no rest;
And when I feign'd an angry look,
    Alas! I loved you best.

Own but the same to me—you'll find
    How blest will be our fate.
O to be happy—to be kind—
    Sure never is too late!

JOHN SHEFFIELD. 1649–1720

Jenny Kissed Me

Jenny kiss'd me when we met,
    Jumping from the chair she sat in;

[35]

Time, you thief, who love to get
    Sweets into your list, put that in!
Say I'm weary, say I'm sad,
    Say that health and wealth have miss'd me,
Say I'm growing old, but add,
    Jenny kiss'd me.

LEIGH HUNT. 1784–1859

When We Two Parted

When we two parted
    In silence and tears,
Half broken-hearted
    To sever for years,
Pale grew thy cheek and cold,
    Colder thy kiss;
Truly that hour foretold
    Sorrow to this.

The dew of the morning
    Sunk chill on my brow—
It felt like the warning
    Of what I feel now.
Thy vows are all broken,
    And light is thy fame:
I hear thy name spoken,
    And share in its shame.

They name thee before me,
    A knell to mine ear;
A shudder comes o'er me—
    Why wert thou so dear?
They know not I knew thee,
    Who knew thee too well:
Long, long shall I rue thee,
    Too deeply to tell.

In secret we met—
    In silence I grieve,

[36]

That thy heart could forget,
  Thy spirit deceive.
If I should meet thee
  After long years,
How should I greet thee?
  With silence and tears.

GEORGE GORDON BYRON, LORD BYRON. 1788–1824

If Thou Must Love Me

If thou must love me, let it be for naught
  Except for love's sake only. Do not say,
  'I love her for her smile—her look—her way
Of speaking gently,—for a trick of thought
That falls in well with mine, and certes brought
  A sense of pleasant ease on such a day'—
  For these things in themselves, Beloved, may
Be changed, or change for thee—and love, so wrought,
May be unwrought so. Neither love me for
  Thine own dear pity's wiping my cheeks dry:
A creature might forget to weep, who bore
  Thy comfort long, and lose thy love thereby!
But love me for love's sake, that evermore
  Thou mayst love on, through love's eternity.

ELIZABETH BARRETT BROWNING. 1806–1861

Now Sleeps the Crimson Petal

  Now sleeps the crimson petal, now the white,
Nor waves the cypress in the palace walk;
Nor winks the gold fin in the porphyry font:
The firefly wakens: waken thou with me.

  Now droops the milk-white peacock like a ghost,
And like a ghost she glimmers on to me.

  Now lies the earth all Danae to the stars,
And all thy heart lies open unto me.

[37]

Now slides the silent meteor on, and leaves
A shining furrow, as thy thoughts in me.

Now folds the lily all her sweetness up,
And slips into the bosom of the lake:
So fold thyself, my dearest, thou, and slip
Into my bosom and be lost in me.

ALFRED, LORD TENNYSON. 1809–1892

Sonnet

Shall I compare thee to a summer's day?
Thou art more lovely and more temperate:
Rough winds do shake the darling buds of May,
And summer's lease hath all too short a date:
Sometime too hot the eye of heaven shines,
And often is his gold complexion dimmed;
And every fair from fair sometime declines,
By chance, or nature's changing course untrimmed;
But thy eternal summer shall not fade,
Nor lose possession of that fair thou owest,
Nor shall death brag thou wander'st in his shade,
When in eternal lines to time thou growest;
    So long as men can breathe, or eyes can see,
    So long lives this, and this gives life to thee.

WILLIAM SHAKESPEARE. 1564–1616

Sonnet

Farewell! thou art too dear for my possessing,
And like enough thou know'st thy estimate:
The charter of thy worth gives thee releasing;
My bonds in thee are all determinate.
For how do I hold thee but by thy granting?
And for that riches where is my deserving?
The cause of this fair gift in me is wanting,
And so my patent back again is swerving.

[38]

Thyself thou gavest, thy own worth then not knowing,
Or me, to whom thou gavest it, else mistaking;
So thy great gift, upon misprision growing,
Comes home again, on better judgment making.
      Thus have I had thee, as a dream doth flatter,
      In sleep a king, but, waking, no such matter.

WILLIAM SHAKESPEARE. 1564–1616

Sonnet

Let me not to the marriage of true minds
Admit impediments. Love is not love
Which alters when it alteration finds,
Or bends with the remover to remove.
O no! it is an ever-fixed mark,
That looks on tempests and is never shaken;
It is the star to every wandering bark,
Whose worth's unknown, although his height be taken.
Love's not Time's fool, though rosy lips and cheeks
Within his bending sickle's compass come;
Love alters not with his brief hours and weeks,
But bears it out ev'n to the edge of doom.
      If this be error, and upon me proved,
      I never writ, nor no man ever loved.

WILLIAM SHAKESPEARE. 1564–1616

Sonnet

Were I as base as is the lowly plain,
And you, my Love, as high as heaven above,
Yet should the thoughts of me, your humble swain,
Ascend to heaven in honour of my love.
Were I as high as heaven above the plain,
And you, my Love, as humble and as low
As are the deepest bottoms of the main,
Wheresoe'er you were, with you my love would go.
Were you the earth, dear Love, and I the skies,

[39]

My love should shine on you like to the Sun,
And look upon you with ten thousand eyes,
Till heaven wax'd blind, and till the world were done.
Wheresoe'er I am—below, or else above you—
Wheresoe'er you are, my heart shall truly love you.

JOSEPH SYLVESTER. 1563–1618

Last Sonnet

Bright Star, would I were steadfast as thou art—
Not in lone splendour hung aloft the night,
And watching, with eternal lids apart,
Like Nature's patient sleepless Eremite,
The moving waters at their priest-like task
Of pure ablution round earth's human shores,
Or gazing on the new soft-fallen mask
Of snow upon the mountains and the moors—
No—yet still steadfast, still unchangeable,
Pillow'd upon my fair love's ripening breast,
To feel for ever its soft fall and swell,
Awake for ever in a sweet unrest,
Still, still to hear her tender-taken breath,
And so live ever—or else swoon to death.

JOHN KEATS. 1795–1821

How Do I Love Thee?

How do I love thee? Let me count the ways.
I love thee to the depth and breadth and height
My soul can reach, when feeling out of sight
For the ends of Being and ideal Grace.
I love thee to the level of every day's
Most quiet need, by sun and candlelight.
I love thee freely, as men strive for Right;
I love thee purely, as they turn from Praise.
I love thee with the passion put to use
In my old griefs, and with my childhood's faith.

I love thee with a love I seemed to lose
With my lost saints,—I love thee with the breath,
Smiles, tears, of all my life!—and, if God choose,
I shall but love thee better after death.

ELIZABETH BARRETT BROWNING. 1806–1861

Where is She Now

Where she is now, I cannot say—
    The world has many a place of light;
Perhaps the sun's eyelashes dance
    On hers, to give them both delight.

Or does she sit in some green shade,
    And then the air that lies above
Can with a hundred pale blue eyes
    Look through the leaves and find my love.

Perhaps she dreams of life with me,
    Her cheek upon her finger-tips;
O that I could leap forward now,
    Behind her back and, with my lips,

Break through those curls above her nape,
    That hover close and lightly there;
To prove if they are substance, or
    But shadows of her lovely hair.

W. H. DAVIES. 1871–1940

The Parting

Since there's no help, come let us kiss and part,—
Nay I have done, you get no more from me;
And I am glad, yea, glad with all my heart,
That thus so cleanly I myself can free;

Shake hands for ever, cancel all our vows,

[41]

And when we meet at any time again,
Be it not seen in either of our brows
That we one jot of former love retain.

Now at the last gasp of Love's latest breath,
When, his pulse failing, Passion speechless lies,
When Faith is kneeling by his bed of death,
And Innocence is closing up his eyes,

—Now if thou would'st, when all have given him over,
From death to life thou might'st him yet recover.

MICHAEL DRAYTON. 1563–1631

To His Coy Mistress

Had we but world enough and time,
This coyness, lady, were no crime.
We would sit down and think which way
To walk, and pass our long love's day.
Thou by the Indian Ganges' side
Shouldst rubies find: I by the tide
Of Humber would complain. I would
Love you ten years before the Flood;
And you should, if you please, refuse
Till the conversion of the Jews.
My vegetable love should grow
Vaster than empires, and more slow.
An hundred years should go to praise
Thine eyes, and on thy forehead gaze;
Two hundred to adore each breast,
But thirty thousand to the rest;
An age at least to every part,
And the last age should show your heart.
For, lady, you deserve this state;
Nor would I love at lower rate.
　　　But at my back I always hear
Time's winged chariot hurrying near;
And yonder all before us lie

Deserts of vast eternity.
Thy beauty shall no more be found;
Nor in thy marble vault shall sound
My echoing song; then worms shall try
That long-preserved virginity;
And your quaint honour turn to dust,
And into ashes all my lust.
The grave's a fine and private place,
But none, I think, do there embrace.
　　　　Now, therefore, while the youthful hue
Sits on thy skin like morning dew,
And while thy willing soul transpires
At every pore with instant fires,
Now, let us sport us while we may;
And now, like amorous birds of prey,
Rather at once our time devour,
Than languish in his slow-chapt power.
Let us roll all our strength, and all
Our sweetness, up into one ball;
And tear our pleasures with rough strife
Thorough the iron gates of life.
Thus, though we cannot make our sun
Stand still, yet we will make him run.

ANDREW MARVELL. 1621–1678

Ye Banks and Braes

Ye banks and braes o' bonnie Doon,
　　　How can ye bloom sae fresh and fair?
How can ye chant, ye little birds,
　　　And I sae weary fu' o' care?
Thou'lt break my heart, thou warbling bird,
　　　That wantons thro' the flowering thorn:
Thou minds me o' departed joys,
　　　Departed never to return.

Aft hae I rov'd by bonnie Doon,
　　　To see the rose and woodbine twine;

[43]

And ilka bird sang o' its love,
    And fondly sae did I o' mine.
Wi' lightsome heart I pu'd a rose,
    Fu' sweet upon its thorny tree;
And my fause lover stole my rose,
    But ah! he left the thorn wi' me.

ROBERT BURNS. 1759–1796

Tam I' The Kirk

O Jean, my Jean, when the bell ca's the congregation
Owre valley an' hill wi' the ding frae its iron mou',
When a'body's thochts is set on his ain salvation,
    Mine's set on you.

There's a reid rose lies on the Buik o' the Word afore ye
That was growin' braw on its bush at the keek o' day,
But the lad that pu'd yon flower i' the mornin's glory,
    He canna pray.

He canna pray; but there's nane i' the kirk will heed him
Whaur he sits sae still his lane at the side o' the wa',
For nane but the reid rose kens what my lassie gie'd him—
    It an' us twa!

He canna sing for the sang that his ain he'rt raises,
He canna see for the mist that's afore his een,
And a voice drouns the hale o' the psalms an' the paraphrases,
    Cryin' 'Jean, Jean, Jean!'

VIOLET JACOB

Down By the Salley Gardens

Down by the salley gardens my love and I did meet;
She passed the salley gardens with little snow-white feet.
She bid me take love easy, as the leaves grow on the tree;
But I, being young and foolish, with her would not agree.

[44]

In a field by the river my love and I did stand,
And on my leaning shoulder she laid her snow-white hand.
She bid me take life easy, as the grass grows on the weirs;
But I was young and foolish, and now am full of tears.

W. B. YEATS. 1865–1938

The Cloths of Heaven

Had I the heavens' embroidered cloths,
    Enwrought with golden and silver light,
The blue and the dim and the dark cloths
Of night and light and the half light,
I would spread the cloths under your feet:
But I, being poor, have only my dreams;
I have spread my dreams under your feet;
Tread softly because you tread on my dreams.

W. B. YEATS. 1865–1938

The Lady's Yes

'Yes!' I answered you last night;
    'No!' this morning, sir, I say!
Colours seen by candle-light
    Will not look the same by day.

When the tabors played their best,
    Lamps above, and laughs below—
Love me sounded like a jest,
    Fit for Yes or fit for No!

Call me false, or call me free—
    Vow, whatever light may shine,
No man on thy face shall see
    Any grief for change on mine.

Yet the sin is on us both—
    Time to dance is not to woo—
Wooer light makes fickle troth—
    Scorn of me recoils on you!

[45]

Learn to win a lady's faith
   Nobly, as the thing is high;
Bravely, as for life and death—
   With a loyal gravity.

Lead her from the festive boards,
   Point her to the starry skies,
Guard her, by your truthful words,
   Pure from courtship's flatteries.

By your truth she shall be true—
   Ever true, as wives of yore—
And her Yes, once said to you,
   SHALL be Yes for evermore.

ELIZABETH BARRETT BROWNING. 1801–1861

Annabel Lee

It was many and many a year ago,
   In a kingdom by the sea,
That a maiden there lived whom you may know
   By the name of ANNABEL LEE;
And this maiden she lived with no other thought
   Than to love and be loved by me.

I was a child and she was a child,
   In this kingdom by the sea:
But we loved with a love that was more than love—
   I and my ANNABEL LEE;
With a love that the winged seraphs of heaven
   Coveted her and me.

And this was the reason that, long ago,
   In this kingdom by the sea,
A wind blew out of a cloud, chilling
   My beautiful ANNABEL LEE;
So that her highborn kinsmen came
   And bore her away from me,

To shut her up in a sepulchre
    In this kingdom by the sea.

The angels, not half so happy in heaven,
    Went envying her and me—
Yes!—that was the reason (as all men know
        In this kingdom by the sea)
That the wind came out of the cloud by night
    Chilling and killing my ANNABEL LEE.

But our love it was stronger by far than the love
    Of those who were older than we—
    Of many far wiser than we—
And neither the angels in heaven above,
    Nor the demons down under the sea,
Can ever dissever my soul from the soul
    Of the beautiful ANNABEL LEE:

For the moon never beams without bringing me dreams
    Of the beautiful ANNABEL LEE;
And the stars never rise but I see the bright eyes
    Of the beautiful ANNABEL LEE;
And so, all the night-tide, I lie down by the side
Of my darling, my darling, my life and my bride,
    In her sepulchre there by the sea—
    In her tomb by the sounding sea.

EDGAR ALLAN POE. 1809–1849

My Old Friend

It seems the world was always bright
    With some divine unclouded weather,
When we, with hearts and footsteps light,
    By lawn and river walked together.

There was no talk of me and you,
    Of theories with facts to bound them,
We were content to be and do,
    And take our fortunes as we found them.

[47]

We spoke no wistful words of love,
    No hint of sympathy and dearness,
Only around, beneath, above,
    There ran a swift and subtle nearness,

Each inmost thought was known to each
    By some impetuous divination:
We found no need of flattering speech,
    Content with silent admiration.

I think I never touched your hand,
    I took no heed of face or feature,
Only, I thought on sea or land
    Was never such a gracious creature.

It seems I was not hard to please,
    Where'er you led I needs must follow;
For strength you were my Hercules,
    For wit and lustre my Apollo.

The years flew onward: stroke by stroke
    They clashed from the impartial steeple,
And we appear to other folk
    A pair of ordinary people.

One word, old friend: though fortune flies,
    I hope should fail—till death shall sever—
In one dim pair of faithful eyes
    You seem as bright, as brave as ever.

ARTHUR C. BENSON

DEATH

D

The Child's Grave

I came to the churchyard where pretty Joy lies
    On a morning in April, a rare sunny day;
Such bloom rose around, and so many birds' cries
    That I sang for delight as I followed the way.

I sang for delight in the ripening of spring,
    For dandelions even were suns come to earth;
Not a moment went by but a new lark took wing
    To wait on the season with melody's mirth.

Love-making birds were my mates all the road,
    And who would wish surer delight for the eye
Than to see goldfinches gleaming abroad
    Or yellow-hammers sunning on paling and sty?

And stocks in the almswomen's garden were blown
    With rich Easter roses each side of the door;
The lazy white owls in the glade cool and lone
    Paid calls on their cousins in the elm's chambered core.

This peace, then, and happiness thronged me around.
    Nor could I go burdened with grief, but made merry
Till I came to the gate of that overgrown ground
    Where scarce once a year sees the priest come to bury.

Over the mounds stood the nettles in pride,
    And, where no fine flowers, there kind weeds dared to
      wave;
It seemed but as yesterday she lay by my side,
    And now my dog ate of the grass on her grave.

He licked my hand wondering to see me muse so,
    And wishes I would lead on the journey or home,
As though not a moment of spring were to go
    In brooding; but I stood, if her spirit might come

And tell me her life, since we left her that day
    In the white lilied coffin, and rained down our tears;
But the grave held no answer, though long I should stay;
    How strange that this clay should mingle with hers!

So I called my good dog, and went on my way;
    Joy's spirit shone then in each flower I went by,
And clear as the noon, in coppice and ley,
    Her sweet dawning smile and her violet eye!

EDMUND BLUNDEN

Early Death

She pass'd away like morning dew
    Before the sun was high;
So brief her time, she scarcely knew
    The meaning of a sigh.

As round the rose its soft perfume,
    Sweet love around her floated;
Admired she grew—while mortal doom
    Crept on, unfear'd, unnoted.

Love was her guardian Angel here,
    But Love to Death resign'd her;
Tho' Love was kind, why should we fear
    But holy Death is kinder?

HARTLEY COLERIDGE. 1796–1849

Remember

Remember me when I am gone away,
    Gone far away into the silent land;
    When you can no more hold me by the hand,
Nor I half turn to go, yet turning stay.
Remember me when no more day by day
    You tell me of our future that you plann'd:

[52]

Only remember me; you understand
It will be late to counsel then or pray.
Yet if you should forget me for a while
    And afterwards remember, do not grieve:
    For if the darkness and corruption leave
    A vestige of the thoughts that once I had,
Better by far you should forget and smile
    Than that you should remember and be sad.

CHRISTINA GEORGINA ROSSETTI. 1830–1894

Dora

She knelt upon her brother's grave,
    My little girl of six years old—
He used to be so good and brave,
    The sweetest lamb of all our fold;
He used to shout, he used to sing,
Of all our tribe the little king—
And so unto the turf her ear she laid,
To hark if still in that dark place he play'd.
    No sound! no sound!
    Death's silence was profound;
    And horror crept
    Into her aching heart, and Dora wept.
    If this is as it ought to be,
    My God, I leave it unto Thee.

THOMAS EDWARD BROWN. 1830–1897

Parted

Farewell to one now silenced quite,
Sent out of hearing, out of sight,—
    My friend of friends, whom I shall miss.
    He is not banished, though, for this,—
Nor he, nor sadness, nor delight.

Thou I shall talk with him no more,
A low voice sounds upon the shore.
>   He must not watch my resting-place,
>   But who shall drive a mournful face
From the sad winds about my door?

I shall not hear his voice complain,
But who shall stop the patient rain?
>   His tears must not disturb my heart,
>   But who shall change the years, and part
The world from every thought of pain?

Although my life is left so dim,
The morning crowns the mountain-rim;
>   Joy is not gone from summer skies,
>   Nor innocence from children's eyes,
And all these things are part of him.

He is not banished, for the showers
Yet wake this green warm earth of ours.
>   How can the summer but be sweet?
>   I shall not have him at my feet,
And yet my feet are on the flowers.

ALICE MEYNELL. 1847–1922

Death, Be Not Proud

Death, be not proud, though some have called thee
Mighty and dreadful, for thou art not so:
For those whom thou think'st thou dost overthrow
Die not, poor Death; nor yet canst thou kill me.
For Rest and Sleep, which but thy pictures be,
Much pleasure, then from thee much more must flow;
And soonest our best men with thee do go—
Rest of their bones and souls' delivery!
Thou'rt slave to fate, chance, kings, and desperate men,
And dost with poison, war and sickness dwell;
And poppy or charms can make us sleep as well

[54]

And better than thy stroke. Why swell'st thou then?
One short sleep past, we wake eternally,
And Death shall be no more: Death, thou shalt die!

JOHN DONNE. 1573–1631

He Could Not Die when Trees were Green

He could not die when trees were green,
For he loved the time too well.
His little hands, when flowers were seen,
Were held for the bluebell,
As he was carried o'er the green.

His eye glanced at the white-nosed bee;
He knew those children of the spring;
When he was well and on the lea
He held one in his hands to sing,
Which filled his heart with glee.

Infants, the children of the Spring!
How can an infant die
When butterflies are on the wing,
Green grass, and such a sky?
How can they die at Spring?

He held his hands for daisies white,
And then for violets blue,
And took them all to bed at night
That in the green fields grew,
As childhood's sweet delight.

And then he shut his little eyes,
And flowers would notice not;
Birds' nests and eggs caused no surprise,
He now no blossoms got:
They met with plaintive sighs.

When Winter came and blasts did sigh,
    And bare were plain and tree,
As he for ease in bed did lie
    His soul seemed with the free,
      He died so quietly.

JOHN CLARE. 1793–1864

Afterwards

When the Present has latched its postern behind my tremulous
    stay,
    And the May month flaps its glad green leaves like wings,
Delicate-filmed as new-spun silk, will the neighbours say,
    'He was a man who used to notice such things'?

If it be in the dusk when, like an eyelid's soundless blink,
    The dewfall-hawk comes crossing the shades to alight
Upon the wind-warped upland thorn, a gazer may think,
    'To him this must have been a familiar sight.'

If I pass during some nocturnal blackness, mothy and warm,
    When the hedgehog travels furtively over the lawn,
One may say, 'He strove that such innocent creatures should come
    to no harm,
    But he could do little for them; and now he is gone.'

If, when hearing that I have been stilled at last, they stand at the
    door,
    Watching the full-starred heavens that winter sees,
Will this thought rise on those who will meet my face no more,
    'He was one who had an eye for such mysteries'?

And will any say when my bell of quittance is heard in the gloom,
    And a crossing breeze cuts a pause in its outrollings,
Till they rise again, as they were a new bell's boom,
    'He hears it not now, but used to notice such things'?

THOMAS HARDY. 1840–1928

Crossing the Bar

Sunset and evening star,
    And one clear call for me!
And may there be no moaning of the bar,
    When I put out to sea,

But such a tide as moving seems asleep,
    Too full for sound and foam,
When that which drew from out the boundless deep
    Turns again home.

Twilight and evening bell,
    And after that the dark!
And may there be no sadness of farewell,
    When I embark;

For tho' from out our bourne of Time and Place
    The flood may bear me far,
I hope to see my Pilot face to face
    When I have crost the bar.

ALFRED, LORD TENNYSON. 1809–1892

The Reaper and the Flowers

There is a Reaper whose name is Death,
    And, with his sickle keen,
He reaps the bearded grain at a breath,
    And the flowers that grow between.

'Shall I have nought that is fair?' saith he;
    'Have nought but the bearded grain?
Though the breath of these flowers is sweet to me
    I will give them all back again.'

[57]

He gazed at the flowers with tearful eyes,
    He kissed their drooping leaves;
It was for the Lord of Paradise
    He bound them in his sheaves.

'My Lord has need of these flowerets gay,'
    The Reaper said, and smiled;
'Dear tokens of the earth are they,
    Where he was once a child.

'They shall all bloom in fields of light,
    Transplanted by my care;
And saints upon their garments white
    These sacred blossoms wear.'

And the mother gave, in tears and pain,
    The flowers she most did love;
She knew she should find them all again
    In the fields of light above.

Oh, not in cruelty, not in wrath,
    The Reaper came that day;
'Twas an angel visited the green earth,
    And took the flowers away.

HENRY W. LONGFELLOW. 1807–1882

Evelyn Hope

I

Beautiful Evelyn Hope is dead!
    Sit and watch by her side an hour.
That is her book-shelf, this is her bed;
    She plucked that piece of geranium-flower,
Beginning to die too, in the glass;
    Little has yet been changed, I think:
The shutters are shut, no light may pass
    Save two long rays thro' the hinge's chink.

[58]

II

Sixteen years old when she died!
    Perhaps she had scarcely heard my name;
It was not her time to love; beside,
    Her life had many a hope and aim,
Duties enough and little cares,
    And now was quiet, now astir,
Till God's hand beckoned unawares,—
    And the sweet white brow is all of her.

III

Is it too late then, Evelyn Hope?
    What, your soul was pure and true,
The good stars met in your horoscope,
    Made you of spirit, fire and dew—
And, just because I was thrice as old
    And our paths in the world diverged so wide,
Each was nought to each, must I be told?
    We were fellow mortals, nought beside?

IV

No, indeed! for God above
    Is great to grant, as mighty to make,
And creates the love to reward the love:
    I claim you still, for my own love's sake!
Delayed it may be for more lives yet,
    Through worlds I shall traverse, not a few:
Much is to learn, much to forget,
    Ere the time be come for taking you.

V

But the time will come, at last it will,
    When, Evelyn Hope, what meant (I shall say)
In the lower earth, in the years long still,
    That body and soul so pure and gay?
Why your hair was amber, I shall divine,
    And your mouth of your own geranium's red—
And what you would do with me, in fine,
    In the new life come in the old one's stead.

VI

I have lived (I shall say) so much since then,
    Given up myself so many times,
Gained me the gains of various men,
    Ransacked the ages, spoiled the climes;
Yet one thing, one, in my soul's full scope,
    Either I missed or itself missed me:
And I want and find you, Evelyn Hope!
    What is the issue? let us see!

VII

I loved you, Evelyn, all the while!
    My heart seemed full as it could hold;
There was place and to spare for the frank young smile,
    And the red young mouth, and the hair's young gold.
So hush,—I will give you this leaf to keep:
    See, I shut it inside the sweet cold hand!
There, that is our secret: go to sleep!
    You will wake, and remember, and understand.

ROBERT BROWNING. 1812–1889

On the Receipt of My Mother's Picture

O that those lips had language! Life has passed
With me but roughly since I heard thee last.
Those lips are thine!—thy own sweet smile I see!
The same, that oft in childhood solaced me;
Voice only fails; else, how distinct they say,
'Grieve not, my child, chase all thy fears away!'
The meek intelligence of those dear eyes
(Blessed be the art that can immortalise,
The art that baffles Time's tyrannic claim
To quench it) here shines on me still the same.
    Faithful remembrancer of one so dear,
O welcome guest, though unexpected here!
Who bidd'st me honour with an artless song,
Affectionate, a mother lost so long.

[60]

I will obey, not willingly alone,
But gladly, as the precept were her own:
And, while that face renews my filial grief,
Fancy shall weave a charm for my relief,
Shall steep me in Elysian reverie,
A momentary dream, that thou art she.
    My mother! when I learnt that thou wast dead,
Say, wast thou conscious of the tears I shed?
Hovered thy spirit o'er thy sorrowing son,
Wretch even then, life's journey just begun?
Perhaps thou gav'st me, though unfelt, a kiss;
Perhaps a tear, if souls can weep in bliss—
Ah, that maternal smile! it answers—Yes.
    I heard the bell tolled on thy burial day,
I saw the hearse that bore thee slow away;
And, turning from my nursery window, drew
A long, long sigh, and wept a last adieu!
But was it such?—It was. Where thou art gone,
Adieus and farewells are a sound unknown—
May I but meet thee on that peaceful shore,
The parting word shall pass my lips no more!
    Thy maidens, grieved themselves at my concern,
Oft gave me promise of thy quick return.
What ardently I wished, I long believed,
And, disappointed still, was still deceived.
By expectation every day beguiled,
Dupe of to-morrow, even from a child.
Thus many a sad to-morrow came and went;
Till, all my stock of infant sorrow spent,
I learned at last submission to my lot;
But, though I less deplored thee, ne'er forgot.
    Where once we dwelt, our name is heard no more,
Children not thine have trod my nursery floor:
And where the gardener Robin, day by day,
Drew me to school along the public way,
Delighted with my bauble coach, and wrapt
In scarlet mantle warm, and velvet capt,
'Tis now become a history little known,
That once we called the pastoral house our own.
Short-lived possession! but the record fair,

That memory keeps of all thy kindness there,
Still outlives many a storm, that has effaced
A thousand other themes less deeply traced.
　　Thy nightly visits to my chamber made,
That thou mightest know me safe, and warmly laid;
Thy morning bounties ere I left my home,
The biscuit, or confectionery plum;
The fragrant waters on my cheeks bestowed
By thy own hand, till fresh they shone and glowed:
All this, and more endearing still than all,
Thy constant flow of love, that knew no fall,
Ne'er roughened by those cataracts and breaks,
That humour interposed too often makes;
All this still legible in memory's page,
And still to be so to my latest age,
Adds joy to duty, makes me glad to pay
Such honours to thee as my numbers may;
—Perhaps a frail memorial, but sincere;
Not scorned in Heaven, though little noticed here.
　　Could Time, his flight reversed, restore the hours
When, playing with thy vesture's tissued flowers—
The violet, the pink, and jessamine,
I pricked them into paper with a pin,
(And thou wast happier than myself the while,
Would softly speak, and stroke my head, and smile)—
Could those few pleasant days again appear—
Might one wish bring them, would I wish them here?
I would not trust my heart—the dear delight
Seems so to be desired, perhaps I might—
But no!—what here we call our life is such—
So little to be loved, and thou so much—
That I should ill requite thee, to constrain
Thy unbound spirit into bonds again.
　　Thou, as a gallant bark from Albion's coast
(The storms all weathered and the ocean crossed)
Shoots into port at some well-havened isle,
Where spices breathe and brighter seasons smile;
There sits quiescent on the floods, that show
Her beauteous form reflected clear below;
While airs, impregnated with incense, play

Around her, fanning light her streamers gay—
So thou—with sails how swift!—hast reached the shore.
'Where tempests never beat, nor billows roar.'
And thy loved consort on the dangerous tide
Of life, long since, has anchored at thy side.
But me, scarce hoping to attain that rest,
Always from port withheld, always distressed—
Me howling winds drive devious, tempest-tossed,
Sails ript, seams opening wide, and compass lost,
And day by day some currents thwarting force
Sets me more distant from a prosperous course,
Yet oh the thought, that thou art safe, and he!
That thought is joy, arrive what may to me.
My boast is not that I deduce my birth
From loins enthroned, and rulers of the earth:
But higher far my proud pretensions rise—
The son of parents passed into the skies.

    And now, farewell—Time unrevoked has run
His wonted course, yet what I wished is done.
By contemplation's help, not sought in vain,
I seem to have lived my childhood o'er again;
To have renewed the joys that once were mine,
Without the sin of violating thine;
And, while the wings of Fancy still are free,
And I can view this mimic show of thee,
Time has but half succeeded in his theft—
Thyself removed, thy power to soothe me left.

WILLIAM COWPER. 1731–1800

The Old Familiar Faces

I have had playmates, I have had companions,
In my days of childhood, in my joyful school-days—
All, all are gone, the old familiar faces.

I have been laughing, I have been carousing,
Drinking late, sitting late, with my bosom cronies—
All, all are gone, the old familiar faces.

[63]

I loved a love once, fairest among women.
Closed are her doors on me, I must not see her—
All, all are gone, the old familiar faces.

I have a friend, a kinder friend has no man.
Like an ingrate, I left my friend abruptly;
Left him, to muse on the old familiar faces.

Ghost-like, I paced round the haunts of my childhood.
Earth seem'd a desert I was bound to traverse,
Seeking to find the old familiar faces.

Friend of my bosom, thou more than a brother!
Why wert not thou born in my father's dwelling?
So might we talk of the old familiar faces.

How some they have died, and some they have left me,
And some are taken from me; all are departed;
All, all are gone, the old familiar faces.

CHARLES LAMB. 1775–1834

The King of Kings

The glories of our blood and state
    Are shadows, not substantial things:
There is no armour against fate:
    Death lays his icy hand on kings:
        Sceptre and crown
        Must tumble down,
And in the dust be equal made
With poor crooked scythe and spade.

Some men with swords may reap the field,
    And plant fresh laurels when they kill,
But their strong nerves at last must yield:
    They tame but one another still.
        Early or late
        They stoop to fate,

And must give up their murmuring breath
When they, pale captives, creep to death.

The garlands wither on their brow—
    Then boast no more your mighty deeds!
Upon Death's purple altar now
    See where the victor-victim bleeds
        All heads must come
        To the cold tomb:
Only the actions of the just
Smell sweet, and blossom in their dust.

JAMES SHIRLEY. 1594–1666

The Wife of Usher's Well

There lived a wife at Usher's Well,
    And a wealthy wife was she;
She had three stout and stalwart sons,
    And sent them to sea.

They hadna been a week from her,
    A week but barely ane,
When word cam' to the carline* wife,
    That her three sons were gane.

They hadna been a week from her,
    A week but barely three,
When word cam' to the carline wife
    That her sons she'd never see.

'I wish the wind may never cease,
    Nor fish be in the flood,
Till my three sons come hame to me,
    In earthly flesh and blood!'

It fell about the Martinmas,
    When nights are lang and mirk,
The carline wife's three sons cam' hame,
    And their hats were o' the birk.†

* Old peasant-woman.   † Birch.

It neither grew in syke* nor ditch,
　　Nor yet in any sheugh;†
But at the gates o' Paradise
　　That birk grew fair eneugh.

'Blow up the fire, my maidens!
　　Bring water from the well!
For a' my house shall feast this night,
　　Since my three sons are well.'

And she has made to them a bed,
　　She's made it large and wide;
And she's ta'en her mantle round about,
　　Sat down at the bedside.

Up then crew the red, red cock,
　　And up and crew the gray:—
The eldest to the youngest said,
　　'Tis time we were away.

'The cock doth craw, the day doth daw,
　　The channerin'‡ worm doth chide;
Gin we be missed out o' our place,
　　A sair pain we maun bide.'

'Lie still, lie still but a little wee while,
　　Lie still but if we may;
Gin my mother should miss us when she wakes
　　She'll go mad ere it be day.

'Our mother has nae mair but us;
　　See where she leans asleep;
The mantle that was on herself
　　She has happed it round our feet.'

O it's they have ta'en up their mother's mantle,
　　And they've hung it on a pin;
'O lang may ye hing, my mother's mantle,
　　Ere ye hap us again!

* Marsh.　　† Trench.　　‡ Fretting.
[66]

'Fare ye weel, my mother dear!
    Fareweel to barn and byre!*
And fare ye weel, the bonny lass
    That kindles my mother's fire!'

ANONYMOUS

Helen of Kirkconnell

I wish I were where Helen lies,
Night and day on me she cries;
O that I were where Helen lies,
    On fair Kirkconnell lea!

Curst be the heart that thought the thought,
And curst the hand that fired the shot,
When in my arms burd Helen dropt,
    And died to succour me!

O thinkna ye my heart was sair
When my love dropt down, and spak' nae mair?
There did she swoon wi' meikle care,
    On fair Kirkconnell lea.

As I went down the water side,
None but my foe to be my guide
None but my foe to be my guide,
    On fair Kirkconnell lea;

I lighted down my sword to draw,
I hacked him in pieces sma',
I hacked him in pieces sma'
    For her sake that died for me.

O Helen fair beyond compare!
I'll mak' a garland o' thy hair,
Shall bind my heart for evermair,
    Until the day I dee!

* Stable.

[67]

O that I were where Helen lies!
Night and day on me she cries;
Out of my bed she bids me rise,
      Says, 'Haste, and come to me!'

O Helen fair! O Helen chaste!
If I were with thee I were blest,
Where thou lies low and takes thy rest,
      On fair Kirkconnell lea.

I wish my grave were growing green,
A winding-sheet drawn ower my e'en,
And I in Helen's arms lying
      On fair Kirkconnell lea,

I wish I were where Helen lies!
Night and day on me she cries,
And I am weary of the skies
      For her sake that died for me.

ANONYMOUS

FOR CHILDREN AND
ABOUT CHILDREN

The Lamplighter

My tea is nearly ready
 and the sun has left the sky;
It's time to take the window
 to see Leerie going by;
For every night at tea-time
 and before you take your seat,
With lantern and with ladder
 he comes posting up the street.

Now Tom would be a driver
 and Maria go to sea,
And my papa's a banker
 and as rich as he can be;
But I, when I am stronger
 and can choose what I'm to do,
O Leerie, I'll go round at night
 and light the lamps with you!

For we are very lucky,
 with a lamp before the door,
And Leerie stops to light it
 as he lights so many more;
And O! before you hurry by
 with ladder and with light,
O Leerie, see a little child
 and nod to him to-night!

ROBERT LOUIS STEVENSON. 1850–1894

My Shadow

I have a little shadow that goes in and out with me,
And what can be the use of him is more than I can see.
He is very, very like me from the heels up to the head;
And I see him jump before me, when I jump into my bed.

[71]

The funniest thing about him is the way he likes to grow—
Not at all like proper children, which is always very slow;
For he sometimes shoots up taller like an india-rubber ball,
And he sometimes gets so little that there's none of him at all.

He hasn't got a notion of how children ought to play,
And can only make a fool of me in every sort of way.
He stays so close beside me, he's a coward you can see;
I'd think shame to stick to nursie as that shadow sticks to me!

One morning, very early, before the sun was up,
I rose and found the shining dew on every buttercup;
But my lazy little shadow, like an arrant sleepy-head,
Had stayed at home behind me and was fast asleep in bed.

ROBERT LOUIS STEVENSON. 1850–1894

The Walrus and the Carpenter

The sun was shining on the sea,
　　Shining with all his might:
He did his very best to make
　　The billows smooth and bright—
And this was odd, because it was
　　The middle of the night.

The moon was shining sulkily,
　　Because she thought the sun
Had got no business to be there
　　After the day was done—
'It's very rude of him,' she said,
　　'To come and spoil the fun!'

The sea was wet as wet could be,
　　The sands were dry as dry.
You could not see a cloud, because
　　No cloud was in the sky:
No birds were flying overhead –
　　There were no birds to fly.

[72]

The Walrus and the Carpenter
  Were walking close at hand:
They wept like anything to see
  Such quantities of sand:
'If this were only cleared away,'
  They said, 'it would be grand!'

'If seven maids with seven mops
  Swept it for half a year,
Do you suppose,' the Walrus said,
  'That they could get it clear?'
'I doubt it,' said the Carpenter,
  And shed a bitter tear.

'O Oysters, come and walk with us!'
  The Walrus did beseech.
'A pleasant walk, a pleasant talk,
  Along the briny beach:
We cannot do with more than four,
  To give a hand to each.'

The eldest Oyster looked at him,
  But not a word he said:
The eldest Oyster winked his eye,
  And shook his heavy head—
Meaning to say he did not choose
  To leave the oyster-bed.

But four young Oysters hurried up,
  All eager for the treat:
Their coats were brushed, their faces washed,
  Their shoes were clean and neat—
And this was odd, because, you know,
  They hadn't any feet.

Four other Oysters followed them,
  And yet another four;
And thick and fast they came at last,
  And more, and more, and more—
All hopping through the frothy waves,
  And scrambling to the shore.

[73]

The Walrus and the Carpenter
  Walked on a mile or so,
And then they rested on a rock
  Conveniently low:
And all the little Oysters stood
  And waited in a row.

'The time has come,' the Walrus said,
  'To talk of many things:
Of shoes—and ships—and sealing wax—
  Of cabbages—and kings—
And why the sea is boiling hot—
  And whether pigs have wings.'

'But wait a bit,' the Oysters cried,
  'Before we have our chat;
For some of us are out of breath,
  And all of us are fat!'
'No hurry!' said the Carpenter.
  They thanked him much for that.

'A loaf of bread,' the Walrus said,
  'Is what we chiefly need:
Pepper and vinegar besides
  Are very good indeed—
Now, if you're ready, Oysters dear,
  We can begin to feed.'

'But not on us!' the Oysters cried,
  Turning a little blue.
'After such kindness that would be
  A dismal thing to do!'
'The night is fine,' the Walrus said,
  'Do you admire the view?

'It was kind of you to come,
  And you are very nice!'
The Carpenter said nothing but
  'Cut us another slice.
I wish you were not quite so deaf—
  I've had to ask you twice!'

'It seems a shame,' the Walrus said,
    'To play them such a trick.
After we've brought them out so far,
    And made them trot so quick!'
The Carpenter said nothing but
    'The butter's spread too thick!'

'I weep for you,' the Walrus said:
    'I deeply sympathize.'
With sobs and tears he sorted out
    Those of the largest size,
Holding his pocket-handkerchief
    Before his streaming eyes.

'O Oysters,' said the Carpenter,
    'You've had a pleasant run!
Shall we be trotting home again?'
    But answer came there none—
And this was scarcely odd, because
    They'd eaten every one.

                    LEWIS CARROLL. 1832–1898

The Wind in a Frolic

The wind one morning sprang up from sleep,
Saying, 'Now for a frolic! now for a leap!
Now for a mad-cap galloping chase!
I'll make a commotion in every place!'

So it swept with a bustle right through a great town,
Cracking the signs and scattering down
Shutters; and whisking, with merciless squalls,
Old women's bonnets and gingerbread stalls.
There never was heard a much lustier shout,
As the apples and oranges trundled about;
And the urchins that stand with their thievish eyes
For ever on watch, ran off each with a prize.

[75]

Then away to the field it went blustering and humming,
And the cattle all wonder'd whatever was coming;
It pluck'd by the tails the grave matronly cows,
And toss'd the colts' manes all over their brows;
Till, offended at such an unusual salute,
They all turn'd their backs, and stood sulky and mute.
So on it went capering and playing its pranks,
Whistling with reeds on the broad river's banks,
Puffing the birds as they sat on the spray,
Or the traveller grave on the king's highway.

It was not too nice to hustle the bags
Of the beggar, and flutter his dirty rags;
'Twas so bold, that it feared not to play its joke
With the doctor's wig or the gentleman's cloak.
Through the forest it roar'd, and cried gaily, 'Now,
You sturdy old oaks, I'll make you bow!'

And it made them bow without much ado,
Or it crack'd their great branches through and through.
Then it rush'd like a monster on cottage and farm,
Striking their dwellings with sudden alarm;
And they ran out like bees in a midsummer swarm.
There were dames with their kerchiefs tied over their caps,
To see if their poultry were free from mishaps;

The turkeys they gobbled, the geese scream'd aloud,
And the hens crept to roost in a terrified crowd;
There was rearing of ladders, and logs laying on,
Where the thatch from the roof threaten'd soon to be gone.
But the wind had swept on, and had met in a lane
With a schoolboy, who panted and struggled in vain;
For it toss'd him, and twirl'd him, then pass'd, and he stood
With his hat in a pool, and his shoes in the mud.

Then away went the wind in its holiday glee,
And now it was far on the billowy sea,
And the lordly ships felt its staggering blow,
And the little boats darted to and fro.

But lo! it was night, and it sank to rest
On the sea-bird's rock in the gleaming west,
Laughing to think, in its fearful fun,
How little of mischief it really had done.

WILLIAM HOWITT. 1795–1879

Letty's Globe

When Letty had scarce pass'd her third glad year,
　　And her young artless words began to flow,
One day we gave the child a colour'd sphere
　　Of the wide earth, that she might mark and know,
By tint and outline, all its sea and land.
　　She patted all the world; old empires peep'd
Between her baby fingers; her soft hand
　　Was welcome at all frontiers. How she leap'd,
　　And laugh'd and prattled in her world-wide bliss;
But when we turn'd her sweet unlearned eye
On our own isle, she raised a joyous cry—
'Oh! yes, I see it, Letty's home is there!'
　　And while she hid all England with a kiss,
Bright over Europe fell her golden hair.

CHARLES TENNYSON TURNER. 1808–1879

Ex Ore Infantium

Little Jesus, wast Thou shy
　　Once, and just so small as I?
And what did it feel like to be
Out of Heaven, and just like me?
Didst Thou sometimes think of there,
And ask where all the angels were?
I should think that I would cry
For my house all made of sky;
I would look about the air,
And wonder where my angels were;
And at waking 'twould distress me—
Not an angel there to dress me!

[77]

Hadst Thou ever any toys,
Like us little girls and boys?
And didst Thou play in Heaven with all
The angels, that were not too tall,
With stars for marbles? Did the things
Play Can you see me? through their wings?
Didst Thou kneel at night to pray,
And didst Thou join Thy hands, this way?
And did they tire sometimes, being young,
And make the prayer seem very long?
And dost Thou like it best, that we
Should join our hands to pray to Thee?
I used to think, before I knew,
The prayer not said unless we do.
And did Thy Mother at the night
Kiss Thee, and fold the clothes in right?
And didst Thou feel quite good in bed,
Kissed, and sweet, and Thy prayers said?

Thou canst not have forgotten all
That it feels like to be small:
And Thou know'st I cannot pray
To Thee in my father's way—
When Thou wast so little, say,
Couldst Thou talk Thy Father's way?—
So, a little Child, come down
And hear a child's tongue like Thy own;
Take me by the hand and walk,
And listen to my baby-talk.

To Thy Father show my prayer
(He will look, Thou art so fair),
And say: 'O Father, I, Thy Son,
Bring the prayer of a little one.'

And He will smile, that children's tongue
Has not changed since Thou wast young.

FRANCIS THOMPSON. 1859–1907

[78]

The Little Black Boy

My mother bore me in the southern wild,
    And I am black, but O, my soul is white!
White as an angel is the English child,
    But I am black, as if bereaved of light.

My mother taught me underneath a tree,
    And, sitting down before the heat of day,
She took me on her lap and kissed me,
    And, pointing to the East, began to say:

'Look at the rising sun: there God does live,
    And gives His light, and gives His heat away,
And flowers and trees and beasts and men receive
    Comfort in morning, joy in the noonday.

'And we are put on earth a little space,
    That we may learn to bear the beams of love;
And these black bodies and this sunburnt face
    Are but a cloud, and like a shady grove.

'For when our souls have learn'd the heat to bear,
    The cloud will vanish, we shall hear His voice,
Saying, "Come out from the grove, my love and care,
    And round my golden tent like lambs rejoice."'

Thus did my mother say, and kissed me,
    And thus I say to little English boy.
When I from black and he from white cloud free,
    And round the tent of God like lambs we joy,

I'll shade him from the heat till he can bear
    To lean in joy upon our Father's knee;
And then I'll stand and stroke his silver hair,
    And be like him, and he will then love me.

WILLIAM BLAKE. 1757–1827

[79]

We Are Seven

——————————A simple child,
That lightly draws its breath,
And feels its life in every limb,
What should it know of death?

I met a little cottage girl:
She was eight years old, she said;
Her hair was thick with many a curl
That clustered round her head.

She had a rustic, woodland air,
And she was wildly clad:
Her eyes were fair, and very fair;
Her beauty made me glad.

'Sisters and brothers, little maid,
How many may you be?'
'How many? Seven in all?' she said,
And wondering looked at me.

'And where are they? I pray you tell.'
She answered, 'Seven are we;
And two of us at Conway dwell,
And two are gone to sea.

'Two of us in the churchyard lie,
My sister and my brother;
And, in the churchyard cottage, I
Dwell near them with my mother.'

'You say that two at Conway dwell,
And two are gone to sea,
Yet ye are seven!—I pray you tell,
Sweet maid, how this may be.'

Then did the little maid reply,
'Seven boys and girls are we;

Two of us in the churchyard lie,
Beneath the churchyard tree.'

'You run about, my little maid,
Your limbs they are alive;
If two are in the churchyard laid,
Then ye are only five.'

'Their graves are green, they may be seen,'
The little maid replied,
'Twelve steps or more from my mother's door,
And they are side by side.

'My stockings there I often knit,
My kerchief there I hem;
And there upon the ground I sit—
I sit and sing to them.

'And often after sunset, sir,
When it is light and fair,
I take my little porringer,
And eat my supper there.

'The first that dies was little Jane;
In bed she moaning lay,
Till God released her of her pain;
And then she went away.

'So in the churchyard she was laid;
And when the grass was dry,
Together round her grave we played,
My brother John and I.

'And when the ground was white with snow,
And I could run and slide,
My brother John was forced to go,
And he lies by her side.'

'How many are you then,' said I,
'If they two are in heaven?'
The little maiden did reply,
'O master! we are seven.'

'But they are dead; those two are dead!
Their spirits are in heaven!'
'Twas throwing words away: for still
The little maid would have her will,
And said, 'Nay, we are seven!'

WILLIAM WORDSWORTH. 1770–1850

The Bishop and the Caterpillar

The Bishop sat in the Schoolmaster's chair:
The Rector, and Curates two were there,
    The Doctor, the Squire,
    The heads of the choir,
And the Gentry around of high degree,
A highly distinguished company;
For the Bishop was greatly beloved in his See!

    And there below,
    A goodly show,
Their faces with soap and with pleasure aglow,
Sat the dear little school-children, row upon row;
For the Bishop had said ('twas the death-blow to schism),
He would hear these dear children their Catechism.
    And then to complete
    The pleasure so sweet
Of these nice little children so pretty and neat,
He'd invited them to a magnificent treat!
And filled were the minds of these dear little ones
With visions of cakes, and of 'gay Sally Lunns,'
Of oceans of tea, and unlimited buns
(The large ones called 'Bath,' not the plain penny ones).

    I think I have read,
    Or at least heard it said:
'Boys are always in mischief, unless they're in bed.'
    I put it to you,
    I don't say it's true,
But if you should ask for my own private view,
I should answer at once, without further ado,

[82]

'I don't think a boy can be trusted to keep
From mischief in bed—unless he's asleep!'

But the Schoolmaster's eye hath a magic spell,
And the boys were behaving remarkably well—
For boys; and the girls—but 'tis needless to say
Their conduct was perfect in every way;
For I'm sure 'tis well known in all ranks of society,
That girls always behave with the utmost propriety.

Now the Bishop arises, and waves his hand;
And the children prepared for his questions stand;
With admiring eyes his form they scan;
He was a remarkably fine-looking man!
His apron was silk of the blackest dye,
His lawn the finest money could buy;
His sleeves and his ruffles than snow were whiter,
He'd his best shovel-hat, and his second-best mitre.
With benignant glance he gazed around—
You might have heard the slightest sound!—
With dignified mien and solemn look
He slowly opened his ponderous book,
And proceeded at once the knowledge to try
Of those nice little children standing by.

   Each child knew its name,
   And who gave it the same,
And all the rest of the questions profound
Which his Lordship was pleased to the school to propound.
Nor less did secular knowledge abound,
For the Bishop, to his great pleasure, found
That they knew the date when our Queen was crowned,
And the number of pence which make up a pound;
And the oceans and seas which our island bound;
That the earth is nearly, but not quite, round;
Their orthography, also, was equally sound,
And the Bishop, at last, completely astound-
   Ed, cried,
   In a tone of pride,
'You bright little dears, no question can trouble you,
You've spelled knife with a k, and wrong with a w.

'And now that my pleasing task's at an end,
I trust you will make of me a friend:
You've answered my questions, and 'tis but fair
That I in replying should take a share;
So if there is aught you would like to know,
Pray ask me about it before I go.
I'm sure it would give me the greatest pleasure
To add to your knowledge, for learning's a treasure
Which you never can lose, and which no one can steal;
It grows by imparting, so do not feel
        Afraid or shy,
        But boldly try,
      Which is the cleverer, you or I!'

Thus amusement with learning judiciously blending,
His Lordship made of his speech an ending,
And a murmur went round of 'How condescending!'

But one bright little boy didn't care a jot
If his Lordship were condescending or not;
        For, with scarce a pause
        For the sounds of applause,
        He raised his head,
        And abruptly said:
      'How many legs has a Caterpillar got?'

Now the Bishop was a learned man,
Bishops always were since the race began,
But his knowledge in that particular line
Was less than yours, and no greater than mine;
And, except that he knew the creature could crawl,
He knew nothing about its legs at all—
Whether the number were great or small,
One hundred, or five, or sixty, or six,—
So he felt in a 'pretty consid'rable fix!'
But, resolving his ignorance to hide,
In measured tones he thus replied:

'The Caterpillar, my dear little boy,
Is an emblem of life and a vision of joy!
It bursts from its shell on a bright green leaf,

[84]

It knows no care, and it feels no grief.'
Then he turned to the Rector and whispered low,
'Mr. Rector, how many? You surely must know.'
But the Rector gravely shook his head,
He hadn't the faintest idea, he said.
So the Bishop turned to the class again,
And in tones paternal took up the strain:
'The Caterpillar, dear children, see,
On its bright green leaf from care lives free,
And it eats, and eats, and grows bigger and bigger,
(Perhaps the Curates can state the figure?)'
But the Curates couldn't; the Bishop went on,
Though he felt that another chance was gone—

'So it eats, and eats, and it grows and grows,
(Just ask the Schoolmaster if he knows).'
But the Schoolmaster said that that kind of knowledge
Was not the sort he had learned at college—
'And when it has eaten enough, then soon
It spins for itself a soft cocoon,
And then it becomes a chrysalis—
I wonder which child can spell me this.
'Tis rather a difficult word to spell—
(Just ask the Schoolmistress if she can tell).'
But the Schoolmistress said, as she shook her grey curls,
'She considered such things were not proper for girls.'

The word was spelled, and spelled quite right,
Those nice little boys were so awfully bright!
And the Bishop began to get into a fright,
His face grew red—it was formerly white—
And the hair on his head stood nearly upright;
He was almost inclined to take refuge in flight,
But he thought that would be too shocking a sight;
He was at his wit's end—nearly—not quite,
For the Pupil-teachers caught his eye.
He thought they might know—as least he would try—
Then he anxiously waited for their reply;
But the Pupil-teachers enjoyed the fun,
And they wouldn't have told if they could have done.

So he said to the Beadle, 'Go down in the street,
And stop all the people you chance to meet,
               I don't care who,
               Any one will do,
The old woman selling lollipops,
The little boys playing with marbles and tops,
Or respectable people who deal at the shops;
The crossing-sweeper, the organ-grinder,
Or the fortune-teller, if you can find her.
               Ask any or all,
               Short or tall,
         Great or small, it matters not—
How many legs has a Caterpillar got?'
The Beadle bowed, and was off like a shot
From a pop-gun fired, or that classical arrow
Which flew from the bow of the wicked cock-sparrow.

Now the Bishop again put on a smile.
And the children, who had been waiting meanwhile,
In their innocent hearts imagined that these
               Remarks applied
               (They were spoken aside)
To the weighty affairs of the diocese.

'The Caterpillar is doomed to sleep
For months—a slumber long and deep.
               Brown and dead
               It looks, 'tis said,
It never even requires to be fed;
And, except that sometimes it waggles its head,
Your utmost efforts would surely fail
To distinguish the creature's head from its tail.

'But one morning in spring,
When the birds loudly sing,
And the earth is gay with blossoming;
When the violets blue
Are wet with dew,
And the sky wears the sweetest cerulean hue!
'When on all is seen
The brightest sheen—

When the daisies are white, and the grass is green;
Then the chrysalis breaks,
The insect awakes,—
To the realms of air its way it takes;
It did not die,
It soars on high,
A bright and beauteous butterfly!'

Here he paused and wiped a tear from his eye;
The Beadle was quietly standing by,
And perceiving the lecture had reached it close,
Whispered, softly and sadly, 'Nobody knows!'

The Bishop saw his last hope was vain,
But to make the best of it he was fain;
So he added, 'Dear children, we ever should be
Prepared to learn from all we see,
And beautiful thoughts of home and joy
Fill the heart, I know, of each girl and boy!
Oh, ponder on these, and you will not care
To know the exact alloted share
Of legs the creature possessed at its birth,
When it crawled a mean worm on this lowly earth.
Yet, if you know it, you now may tell,
Your answers so far have pleased me well.'

Then he looked around with benignant eye,
Nor long did he wait for the reply,
For the bright little boy, with a countenance gay,
Said, 'Six, for I counted 'em yesterday!'

MORAL

'To all who have children under their care,'
Of two things, nay, three things, I pray you beware—
Don't give them too many 'unlimited buns,'
Six each (Bath) is sufficient or twelve penny ones;
Don't let them go in for examination,
Unless you have given them due preparation,
Or the questions, asked with the kindest intention,
May be rather a strain on their powers of invention.

[87]

Don't pretend you know everything under the sun,
Though your school-days are ended, and theirs but begun,
But honestly say, when the case is so,
'This thing, my dear children, I do not know':
For they really must learn, either slower or speedier,
That you're not a walking Encyclopædia!

MARY E. MANNERS

Human Nature

Two little children five years old,
Marie the gentle, Charlie the bold;
Sweet and bright and quaintly wise,
Angels both, in their mother's eyes.

But you, if you follow my verse, shall see,
That they were as human as human can be,
And had not yet learned the maturer art
Of hiding the 'self' of the finite heart.

One day they found in their romp and play
Two little rabbits soft and grey—
Soft and grey, and just of a size,
As like each other as your two eyes.

All day long the children made love
To their dear little pets—their treasure-trove
They kissed and hugged them until the night
Brought to the conies a glad respite.

Too much fondling doesn't agree
With the rabbit nature, as we shall see,
For ere the light of another day
Had chased the shadows of night away,

One little pet had gone to the shades,
Or, let us hope, to perennial glades
Brighter and softer than any below—
A heaven where good little bunnies go.

[88]

The living and dead lay side by side,
And still alike as before one died;
And it chanced that the children came singly to view
The pets they had dreamed of the whole night through.

First came Charlie, and, with sad surprise,
Beheld the dead with streaming eyes;
Howe'er, consolingly, he said,
'Poor little Marie—her rabbit's dead!'

Later came Marie, and stood aghast;
She kissed and caressed it, but at last
Found voice to say, while her young heart bled,
'I'm sorry for Charlie—his rabbit's dead!'

Two little children, quaintly wise,
Angels both in their mother's eyes,
But you having followed my tale can see
That they were as human as human can be!

ANONYMOUS

Indoor Games Near Newbury

In among the silver birches winding ways of tarmac wander
  And the signs to Bussock Bottom, Tussock Wood and Windy
    Brake,
Gabled lodges, tile-hung churches, catch the lights of our Lagonda
  As we drive to Wendy's party, lemon curd and Christmas cake.
Rich the makes of motor whirring, past the pine-plantation pur-
    ring
              Come up, Hupmobile, Delage!
Short the way your chauffeurs travel, crunching over private
    gravel
              Each from out his warm garage.

Oh but Wendy, when the carpet yielded to my indoor pumps
  There you stood, your gold hair streaming, handsome in the
    hall light gleaming

[89]

There you looked and there you led me off into the game of
    clumps
  Then the new Victrola playing and your funny uncle saying
'Choose your partners for a fox-trot! Dance until it's tea o'clock!
  'Come on, young 'uns, foot it featly!' Was it chance that paired
    us neatly,
            I, who loved you so completely,
You, who pressed me closely to you, hard against your party
    frock?

'Meet me when you've finished eating!' So we met and no one
    found us.
  Oh that dark and furry cupboard while the rest played hide and
    seek!
Holding hands our two hearts beating in the bedroom silence
    round us,
  Holding hands and hardly hearing sudden footstep, thud and
    shriek.
Love that lay too deep for kissing—'Where is Wendy? Wendy's
    missing!'
            Love so pure it had to end,
Love so strong that I was frighten'd when you gripped my fingers
    tight and
            Hugging, whispered 'I'm your friend.'

Good-bye Wendy! Send the fairies, pinewood elf and larch tree
    gnome,
  Spingle-spangled stars are peeping at the lush Lagonda creeping
Down the winding ways of tarmac to the leaded lights of home.
  There, among the silver birches, all the bells of all the churches
Sounded in the bath-waste running out into the frosty air.
  Wendy speeded my undressing, Wendy is the sheet's caressing
            Wendy bending gives a blessing,
Holds me as I drift to dreamland, safe inside my slumberwear.

                                    JOHN BETJEMAN

NATURE

Autumn Evening

The shadows flickering, the daylight dying,
And I upon the old red sofa lying,
The great brown shadows leaping up the wall,
The sparrows twittering; and that is all.

I thought to send my soul to far-off lands,
Where fairies scamper on the windy sands,
Or where the autumn rain comes drumming down
On huddled roofs in an enchanted town.

But O my sleepy soul, it will not roam,
It is too happy and too warm at home:
With just the shadows leaping up the wall,
The sparrows twittering; and that is all.

FRANCES CORNFORD

Weathers

This is the weather the cuckoo likes,
    And so do I;
When showers betumble the chestnut spikes,
    And nestlings fly:
And the little brown nightingale bills his best,
And they sit outside at 'The Travellers' Rest',
And maids come forth sprig-muslin drest,
And citizens dream of the south and west,
    And so do I.

This is the weather the shepherd shuns,
    And so do I;
When beeches drip in browns and duns,
    And thresh, and ply;
And hill-hid tides throb, throe on throe,
And meadow rivulets overflow,

And drops on gate-bars hang in a row,
And rooks in families homeward go,
    And so do I.

THOMAS HARDY. 1840–1928

May Morning—Colour of Lilac

Colour of lilac
    And laburnum gold,
    Candles of chestnut
Lighted by the Spring,
Greenfinches unseen,
Lulling the tranquil hours,
Sheep voices from the fold
And swallows on the wing.

Bespangled meadows
And green willows blithe,
Small orchards blossom-clad,
The hedgerows white with may;
Old men a-talking
As the long grass falls
Before the swishing scythe,
And white-frocked girls at play.

Cuckoos calling
In the woods at morn,
Wallflowers basking
Round the sunken pool,
Windows opening
To far hillsides
Green with growing corn;
Smooth lawns all shadow-cool.

Reed-fringed river
Where the iris grows
And cows contented stand
In heat of day;

Long silent lanes
Whose cloistering hedges
Borrow the first wild rose
From June, for May.

D. LOVATT WILLIAMS

Corinna's Going A-Maying

Get up, get up for shame! The blooming morn
    Upon her wings presents the gold unshorn.
        See how Aurora throws her fair
        Fresh-quilted colours through the air:
        Get up, sweet slug-a-bed, and see
        The dew bespangling herb and tree!
Each flower has wept and bow'd toward the east
Above an hour since, yet you not drest;
        Nay! not so much as out of bed?
        When all the birds have matins said
        And sung their thankful hymns, 'tis sin,
        Nay, profanation, to keep in,
Whenas a thousand virgins on this day
Spring sooner than the lark, to fetch in May.

Rise and put on your foliage, and be seen
To come forth, like the spring-time, fresh and green,
        And sweet as Flora. Take no care
        For jewels for your gown or hair:
        Fear not; the leaves will strew
        Gems in abundance upon you:
Besides, the childhood of the day has kept,
Against you come, some orient pearls unwept.
        Come, and receive them while the light
        Hangs on the dew-locks of the night:
        And Titan on the eastern hill
        Retires himself, or else stands still
Till you come forth! Wash, dress, be brief in praying:
Few beads* are best when once we go a-Maying.

* Beads, prayers.

Come, my Corinna, come; and coming, mark
How each field turns a street, each street a park,
    Made green and trimm'd with trees! see how
    Devotion gives each house a bough
    Or branch! each porch, each door, ere this,
    An ark, a tabernacle is,
Made up of white-thorn neatly interwove,
As if here were those cooler shades of love.
    Can such delights be in the street
    And open fields, and we not see't?
    Come, we'll abroad: and let's obey
    The proclamation made for May,
And sin no more, as we have done, by staying;
But, my Corinna, come, let's go a-Maying.

There's not a budding boy or girl this day
But is got up and gone to bring in May.
    A deal of youth, ere this, is come
    Back, and with white-thorn laden home.
    Some have despatch'd their cakes and cream,
    Before that we have left to dream:
And some have wept and woo'd, and plighted troth,
And chose their priest, ere we can cast off sloth:
    Many a green-gown† has been given,
    Many a kiss, both odd and even:
    Many a glance, too, has been sent
    From out the eye, love's firmament:
Many a jest told of the keys betraying
This night, and locks pick'd: yet we're not a-Maying!

† Green-grown, tumble on the grass.

Come, let us go, while we are in our prime,
And take the harmless folly of the time!
    We shall grow old apace, and die
    Before we know our liberty.
    Our life is short, and our days run
    As fast away as does the sun.
And, as a vapour or a drop of rain,
Once lost, can ne'er be found again,
    So when or you or I are made

[96]

A fable, song, or fleeting shade,
All love, all liking, all delight
Lies drown'd with us in endless night.
Then, while time serves, and we are but decaying,
Come, my Corinna, come, let's go a-Maying.

ROBERT HERRICK. 1591–1674

To Autumn

Season of mists and mellow fruitfulness!
  Close bosom-friend of the maturing sun;
Conspiring with him how to load and bless
  With fruit the vines that round the thatch-eaves run;
To bend with apples the moss'd cottage-trees,
  And fill all fruit with ripeness to the core;
    To swell the gourd, and plump the hazel shells
With a sweet kernel; to set budding more,
And still more, later flowers for the bees,
Until they think warm days will never cease,
    For Summer has o'er-brimmed their clammy cells.

Who hath not seen thee oft amid thy store?
  Sometimes whoever seeks abroad may find
Thee sitting careless on a granary floor,
  Thy hair soft-lifted by the winnowing wind;
Or on a half-reap'd furrow sound asleep,
  Drowsed with the fume of poppies, while thy hook
    Spares the next swath and all its twined flowers;
And sometimes like a gleaner thou dost keep
  Steady thy laden head across a brook;
  Or by a cider-press, with patient look,
    Thou watchest the last oozings, hours by hours.

Where are the songs of Spring? Ay, where are they?
  Think not of them, thou hast they music too,—
While barred clouds bloom the soft-dying day,
  And touch the stubble-plains with rosy hue;
Then in a wailful choir the small gnats mourn

G

Among the river sallows, borne aloft
Or sinking as the light wind lives or dies;
And full-grown lambs loud bleat from hilly bourn;
Hedge-crickets sing; and now with treble soft
The red-breast whistles from a garden-croft,
And gathering swallows twitter in the skies.

JOHN KEATS. 1795–1821

The Storm

I stood on the lonely beach below
And gazed into the sky,
I heard the waves lash on the shore
And the seagull's plaintive cry.

The clouds were thick and darker now,
The foaming waves were strong.
The wind whipped up the golden sand
As I fought my way along.

A flash of lightning pierced the sky,
A roll of thunder came.
I hurried quickly to my home
To shelter from the rain.

But then the rain stopped suddenly,
The waves upon the shore
Grew calm, the mighty wind died down,
And all was peace once more.

JILL JELLICOE
(from Liverpool, age 12 years)

To a Bull-Dog

We shan't see Willy any more, Mamie,
He won't be coming any more:
He came back once and again and again,
But he won't get leave any more.

[98]

We looked from the window and there was his cab,
    And we ran downstairs like a streak,
And he said 'Hullo, you bad dog,' and you crouched to the floor,
    Paralysed to hear him speak,

And then let fly at his face and his chest
    Till I had to hold you down,
While he took off his cap and his gloves and his coat.
    And his bag and his thonged Sam Browne.

We went upstairs to the studio,
    The three of us, just as of old,
And you lay down and I sat and talked to him
    As round the room he strolled.

Here in the room where, years ago
    Before the old life stopped,
He worked all day with his slippers and his pipe,
    He would pick up the threads he'd dropped,

Fondling all the drawings he had left behind,
    Glad to find them all still the same,
And opening the cupboards to look at his belongings
. . . Every time he came.

But now I know what a dog doesn't know,
    Though you'll thrust your head on my knee,
And try to draw me from the absent-mindedness
    That you find so dull in me.

And all your life you will never know
    What I wouldn't tell you even if I could,
That the last time we waved him away
    Willy went for good.

But sometimes as you lie on the hearthrug
    Sleeping in the warmth of the stove,
Even through your muddled old canine brain
    Shapes from the past may rove.

[99]

You'll scarcely remember, even in a dream,
  How we brought home a silly little pup,
With a big square head and little crooked legs
  That could scarcely bear him up,

But your tail will tap at the memory
  Of a man whose friend you were,
Who was always kind though he called you a naughty dog
  When he found you on his chair;

Who'd make you face a reproving finger
  And solemnly lecture you
Till your head hung downwards and you looked very sheepish!
  And you'll dream of your triumphs too.

Of summer evening chases in the garden
  When you dodged us all about with a bone:
We were three boys, and you were the cleverest,
  But now we're two alone.

When summer comes again,
  And the long sunsets fade,
We shall have to go on playing the feeble game for two
  That since the war we've played.

And though you run expectant as you always do
  To the uniforms we meet,
You'll never find Willy among all the soldiers
  In even the longest street,

Nor in any crowd; yet, strange and bitter thought,
  Even now were the old words said,
If I tried the old trick and said 'Where's Willy?'
  You would quiver and lift your head,

And your brown eyes would look to ask if I were serious,
  And wait for the word to spring.
Sleep undisturbed: I shan't say that again,
  You innocent old thing.

[100]

I must sit, not speaking, on the sofa,
   While you lie asleep on the floor;
For he's suffered a thing that dogs couldn't dream of,
   And he won't be coming here any more.

SIR JOHN SQUIRE

Ode On the Death of a Favourite Cat

'Twas on a lofty vase's side,
   Where China's gayest art had dy'd
The azure flowers, that blow;
Demurest of the tabby kind,
The pensive Selima reclin'd,
   Gazed on the lake below.

Her conscious tail her joy declar'd;
The fair round face, the snowy beard,
   The velvet of her paws,
Her coat, that with the tortoise vies,
Her ears of jet, and emerald eyes,
   She saw; and purr'd applause.

Still had she gaz'd; but 'midst the tide
Two angel forms were seen to glide,
   The Genii of the stream:
Their scaly armour's Tyrian hue
Thro' richest purple to the view
   Betray'd a golden gleam.

The hapless Nymph with wonder saw:
A whisker first and then a claw,
   With many an ardent wish,
She stretch'd in vain to reach the prize.
What female heart can gold despise?
   What Cat's averse to fish?

Presumptuous Maid! with looks intent
Again she stretch'd, again she bent,
   Nor knew the gulf between.

(Malignant Fate sat by, and smil'd)
The slipp'ry verge her feet beguil'd,
   She tumbled headlong in.

Eight times emerging from the flood
She mew'd to ev'ry watry God,
   Some speedy aid to send.
No Dolphin came, no Nereid stirr'd:
Nor cruel Tom, nor Susan heard.
   A Fav'rite has no friend!

From hence, ye Beauties, undeceiv'd,
Know, one false step is ne'er retriev'd,
   And be with caution bold.
Not all that tempts your wand'ring eyes
And heedless hearts, is lawful prize;
   Nor all, that glisters, gold.

THOMAS GRAY. 1716–1771

The Oxen

Christmas Eve, and twelve of the clock.
   'Now they are all on their knees,'
An elder said as we sat in a flock
   By the embers in hearthside ease.

We pictured the meek mild creatures where
   They dwelt in their strawy pen,
Nor did it occur to one of us there
   To doubt they were kneeling then.

So fair a fancy few believe
   In these years! Yet, I feel,
If someone said on Christmas Eve
   'Come; see the oxen kneel

In the lonely barton by yonder coomb
   Our childhood used to know,'
I should go with him in the gloom,
   Hoping it might be so.

THOMAS HARDY. 1840–1928

Ode to a Nightingale

My heart aches, and a drowsy numbness pains
    My sense, as though of hemlock I had drunk,
Or emptied some dull opiate to the drains
    One minute past, and Lethe-wards had sunk:
'Tis not through envy of thy happy lot,
    But being too happy in thine happiness,—
        That thou, light-winged Dryad of the trees,
           In some melodious plot,
    Of beechen green, and shadows numberless,
    Singest of summer in full-throated ease.

O for a draught of vintage, that hath been
    Cooled a long age in the deep-delved earth,
Tasting of Flora and the country green,
    Dance, and Provencal song, and sunburnt mirth!
O for a beaker full of the warm South,
    Full of the true, the blushful Hippocrene,
        With beaded bubbles winking at the brim,
           And purple-stained mouth!
That I might drink, and leave the world unseen,
    And with thee fade away into the forest dim:

Fade far away, dissolve, and quite forget
    What thou amongst the leaves hast never known,
The weariness, the fever, and the fret
    Here, where men sit and hear each other groan;
Where palsy shakes a few, sad, last gray hairs,
    Where youth grows pale, and spectre-thin, and dies;
        Where but to think is to be full of sorrow
           And leadened-eyed despairs;
    Where beauty cannot keep her lustrous eyes,
    Or new Love pine at them beyond to-morrow.

Away! away! for I will fly to thee,
    Not charioted by Bacchus and his pards,
But on the viewless wings of Poesy,

Though the dull brain perplexes and retards.
Already with thee! tender is the night,
    And haply the Queen-Moon is on her throne,
        Clustered around by all her starry Fays;
            But here there is no light,
Save what from heaven is with the breezes blown
    Through verdurous glooms and winding mossy ways.

I cannot see what flowers are at my feet,
    Nor what soft incense hangs upon the boughs,
But, in embalmed darkness, guess each sweet
    Wherewith the seasonable month endows
The grass, the thicket, and the fruit-tree wild;
    White hawthorn, and the pastoral eglantine;
        Fast fading violets covered up in leaves;
            And mid-May's eldest child,
    The coming musk-rose, full of dewy wine,
        The murmurous haunt of flies on summer eves.

Darkling I listen; and for many a time
    I have been half in love with easeful Death,
Called him soft names in many a mused rhyme,
    To take into the air my quiet breath;
Now more than ever seems it rich to die,
    To cease upon the midnight with no pain
        While thou art pouring forth thy soul abroad
            In such an ecstasy!
    Still wouldst thou sing, and I have ears in vain—
        To thy high requiem become a sod.

Thou wast not born for death, immortal Bird!
    No hungry generations tread thee down;
The voice I hear this passing night was heard
    In ancient days by emperor and clown:
Perhaps the self-same song that found a path
    Through the sad heart of Ruth, when, sick for home,
        She stood in tears amid the alien corn;
            The same that oft-times hath
    Charmed magic casements, opening on the foam
        Of perilous seas, in faery lands forlorn.

[104]

Forlorn! the very word is like a bell
 To toll me back from thee to my sole self.
Adieu! the fancy cannot cheat so well
 As she is famed to do, deceiving elf.
Adieu! adieu! thy plaintive anthem fades
 Past the near meadows, over the still stream,
  Up the hill-side; and now 'tis buried deep
  In the next valley-glades:
 Was it a vision, or a waking dream?
 Fled is that music:—do I wake or sleep?

JOHN KEATS. 1795–1821

The Cuckoo

 O blithe New-comer! I have heard,
  I hear thee and rejoice.
 O Cuckoo! Shall I call thee Bird,
  Or but a wandering voice?

 While I am lying on the grass
  Thy twofold shout I hear;
 From hill to hill it seems to pass
  At once far off, and near.

 Though babbling only to the Vale,
  Of sunshine and of flowers,
 Thou bringest unto me a tale
  Of visionary hours.

 Thrice welcome, darling of the spring!
  Even yet thou art to me
 No bird, but an invisible thing,
  A voice, a mystery;

 The same whom in my schoolboy days
  I listened to; that Cry
 Which made me look a thousand ways
  In bush, and tree, and sky.

To seek thee did I often rove
    Through woods and on the green;
And thou wert still a hope, a love;
    Still longed for, never seen.

And I can listen to thee yet;
    Can lie upon the plain
And listen, till I do beget
    That golden time again.

O blessed Bird! the earth we pace
    Again appears to be
An unsubstantial, faery place
    That is fit home for thee!

WILLIAM WORDSWORTH. 1770–1850

The Retired Cat

A Poet's cat, sedate and grave,
As poet well could wish to have,
Was much addicted to inquire
For nooks, to which she might retire,
And where, secure as mouse in chink,
She might repose, or sit and think.
I know not where she caught the trick—
Nature perhaps herself had cast her
In such a mould PHILOSOPHIQUE,
Or else she learn'd it of her master.
Sometimes ascending, debonair,
An apple-tree or lofty pear,
Lodg'd with convenience in the fork,
She watched the gard'ner at his work;
Sometimes her ease and solace sought
In an old empty wat'ring pot,
There wanting nothing, save a fan,
To seem some nymph in her sedan,
Apparell'd in exactest sort,
And ready to be borne to court.

[106]

But love of change it seems has place
Not only in our wiser race;
Cats also feel as well as we
That passion's force, and so did she.
Her climbing, she began to find,
Expos'd her too much to the wind,
And the old utensil of tin
Was cold and comfortless within:
She therefore wish'd instead of those,
Some place of more serene repose,
Where neither cold might come, nor air
Too rudely wanton with her hair,
And sought it in the likeliest mode
Within her master's snug abode.

A draw'r,—it chanc'd, at bottom lin'd
With linen of the softest kind,
With such as merchants introduce
From India, for the ladies' use,—
A draw'r impending o'er the rest,
Half open in the topmost chest,
Of depth enough, and none to spare,
Invited her to slumber there.
Puss with delight beyond expression,
Survey'd the scene, and took possession.
Recumbent at her ease ere long,
And lull'd by her own hum-drum song,
She left the cares of life behind,
And slept as she would sleep her last,
When in came, housewifely inclin'd,
The chambermaid, and shut it fast,
By no malignity impell'd,
But all unconscious whom it held.

Awaken'd by the shock (cried puss)
Was ever cat attended thus!
The open draw'r was left, I see,
Merely to prove a nest for me,
For soon as I was well compos'd,
Then came the maid, and it was closed:
How smooth these 'kerchiefs, and how sweet,
O what a delicate retreat!

I will resign myself to rest
Till Sol, declining in the west,
Shall call to supper; when, no doubt,
Susan will come and let me out.
   The evening came, the sun descended,
And puss remain'd still unattended.
The night roll'd tardily away,
(With her indeed 'twas never day)
The sprightly morn her course renew'd,
The evening gray again ensued,
And puss came into mind no more
Than if entomb'd the day before.
With hunger pinch'd, and pinch'd for room,
She now presag'd approaching doom,
Not slept a single wink, or purr'd,
Conscious of jeopardy incurr'd.
   That night, by chance, the poet watching,
Heard an inexplicable scratching,
His noble heart went pit-a-pat,
And to himself he said—what's that?
He drew the curtain at his side,
And forth he peep'd, but nothing spied.
Yet, by his ear directed, guess'd
Something imprison'd in the chest,
And doubtful what, with prudent care,
Resolv'd it should continue there.
At length a voice, which well he knew,
A long and melancholy mew,
Saluting his poetic ears,
Consol'd him, and dispell'd his fears;
He left his bed, he trod the floor,
He 'gan in haste the draw'rs explore,
The lowest first, and without stop,
The rest in order to the top.
For 'tis a truth well known to most,
That whatsoever thing is lost,
We seek it, ere it comes to light,
In ev'ry cranny but the right.
Forth skipp'd the cat; not now replete
As erst with airy self-conceit,

Nor in her own fond apprehension,
A theme for all the world's attention,
But modest, sober, cur'd of all
Her notions hyberbolical,
And wishing for a place of rest
Any thing rather than a chest:
Then stept the poet into bed,
With this reflexion in his head:

MORAL

Beware of too sublime a sense
Of your own worth and consequence!
The man who dreams himself so great,
And his importance of such weight,
That all around, in all that's done,
Must move and act for him alone,
Will learn, in school of tribulation,
The folly of his expectation.

WILLIAM COWPER. 1731–1800

Tyger! Tyger! Burning Bright

Tyger! tyger! burning bright
In the forests of the night,
What immortal hand or eye
Could frame thy fearful symmetry?

In what distant deeps or skies
Burnt the fire of thine eyes?
On what wings dare he aspire?
What the hand dare seize the fire?

And what shoulder, and what art,
Could twist the sinews of thy heart?
And when thy heart began to beat
What dread hand? and what dread feet?

What the hammer? what the chain?
In what furnace was thy brain?
What the anvil? what dread grasp
Dare its deadly terrors clasp?

When the stars threw down their spears,
And water'd heaven with their tears,
Did he smile his work to see?
Did he who made the lamb make thee?

Tyger! tyger! burning bright
In the forests of the night,
What immortal hand or eye,
Dare frame thy fearful symmetry?

WILLIAM BLAKE. 1757–1827

Ducks

I

From troubles of the world
    I turn to ducks,
Beautiful comical things
Sleeping or curled
Their heads beneath white wings
By water cool,
Or finding curious things
To eat in various mucks
Beneath the pool,
Tails uppermost, or waddling
Sailor-like on the shores
Of ponds, or paddling
—Left! right!—with fanlike feet
Which are for steady oars
When they (white galleys) float
Each bird a boat
Rippling at will the sweet
Wide waterway . . .
When night is fallen you creep

[110]

Upstairs, but drakes and dillies
Nest with pale water-stars,
Moonbeams and shadow bars,
And water-lilies:
Fearful too much to sleep
Since they've no locks
To click against the teeth
Of weasel and fox.
And warm beneath
Are eggs of cloudy green
Whence hungry rats and lean
Would stealthily suck
New life, but for the mien,
The bold ferocious mien
Of the mother-duck.

II

Yes, ducks are valiant things
On nests of twigs and straws,
And ducks are soothy things
And lovely on the lake
When that the sunlight draws
Thereon their pictures dim
In colours cool.
And when beneath the pool
They dabble, and when they swim
And make their rippling rings,
O ducks are beautiful things!
But ducks are comical things:—
As comical as you.
Quack!
They waddle round, they do.
They eat all sorts of things,
And then they quack.
By barn and stable and stack
They wander at their will,
But if you go too near
They look at you through black
Small topaz-tinted eyes

And wish you ill.
Triangular and clear
They leave their curious track
In mud at the water's edge,
And there amid the sedge
And slime they gobble and peer
Saying 'Quack! quack!'

III

When God had finished the stars and whirl of coloured suns
He turned His mind from big things to fashion little ones,
Beautiful tiny things (like daisies) He made, and then
He made the comical ones in case the minds of men
        Should stiffen and become
        Dull, humourless and glum:
And so forgetful of their Maker be
As to take even themselves—quite seriously.
Caterpillars and cats are lively and excellent puns:
All God's jokes are good—even the practical ones!
And as for the duck, I think God must have smiled a bit
Seeing those bright eyes blink on the day He fashioned it.
And He's probably laughing still at the sound that came out of
    its bill!

F. W. HARVEY

The Darkling Thrush

I leant upon a coppice gate
    When Frost was spectre-gray,
And Winter's dregs made desolate
    The weakening eye of day.
The tangled bine-stems scored the sky
    Like strings from broken lyres,
And all mankind that haunted nigh
    Had sought their household fires.

The land's sharp features seemed to be
    The Century's corpse outleant,

His crypt the cloudy canopy,
    The wind his death-lament.
The ancient pulse of germ and birth
    Was shrunken hard and dry,
And every spirit upon earth
    Seemed fervourless as I.

At once a voice burst forth among
    The bleak twigs overhead
In a full-hearted evensong
    Of joy illimited;
An aged thrush, frail, gaunt, and small,
    In blast-beruffled plume,
Had chosen thus to fling his soul
    Upon the growing gloom.

So little cause for carollings
    Of such ecstatic sound
Was written on terrestrial things
    Afar or nigh around,
That I could think there trembled through
    His happy good-night air
Some blessed Hope, whereof he knew
    And I was unaware.

THOMAS HARDY. 1840–1928

The Bells of Heaven

'Twould ring the bells of Heaven
    The wildest peal for years,
If Parson lost his senses
And people came to theirs,
And he and they together
Knelt down with angry prayers
For tamed and shabby tigers,
And dancing dogs and bears,
And wretched, blind pit-ponies,
And little hunted hares.

RALPH HODGSON

The Snare

I hear a sudden cry of pain!
    There is a rabbit in a snare:
Now I hear the cry again,
    But I cannot tell from where.

But I cannot tell from where
    He is calling out for aid;
Crying on the frightened air,
    Making everything afraid.

Making everything afraid,
    Wrinkling up his little face,
As he cries again for aid;
    And I cannot find the place!

And I cannot find the place
    Where his paw is in the snare:
Little one! Oh, little one!
    I am searching everywhere.

JAMES STEPHENS

Milk for the Cat

When the tea is brought at five o'clock,
    And all the neat curtains are drawn with care,
The little black cat with bright green eyes
Is suddenly purring there.

At first she pretends, having nothing to do,
She has come in merely to blink by the grate,
But, though tea may be late or the milk may be sour,
She is never late.

And presently her agate eyes
Take a soft large milky haze,

And her independent casual glance
Becomes a stiff hard gaze.

Then she stamps her claws or lifts her ears,
Or twists her tail and begins to stir,
Till suddenly all her lithe body becomes
One breathing trembling purr.

The children eat and wriggle and laugh;
The two old ladies stroke their silk:
But the cat is grown small and thin with desire,
Transformed to a creeping lust for milk.

The white saucer like some full moon descends—
At last from the clouds of the table above;
She sighs and dreams and thrills and glows,
Transfigured with love.

She nestles over the shining rim,
Buries her chin in the creamy sea;
Her tail hangs loose; each drowsy paw—
Is doubled under each bending knee.

A long dim ecstasy holds her life;
Her world is an infinite shapeless white,
Till her tongue has curled the last holy drop,
Then she sinks back into the night,

Draws and dips her body to heap
Her sleepy nerves in the great arm-chair,
Lies defeated and buried deep
Three or four hours unconscious there.

HAROLD MONRO. 1879–1932

The Donkey

When fishes flew and forests walked
    And figs grew upon thorn,
Some moment when the moon was blood
    Then surely I was born;

[115]

With monstrous head and sickening cry
  And ears like errant wings,
The devil's walking parody
  On all four-footed things.

The tattered outlaw of the earth,
  Of ancient crooked will;
Starve, scourge, deride me: I am dumb,
  I keep my secret still.

Fools! For I also had my hour;
  One far fierce hour and sweet:
There was a shout about my ears,
  And palms before my feet.

GILBERT KEITH CHESTERTON. 1872–1936

Tim, an Irish Terrier

It's wonderful dogs they're breeding now:
  Small as a flea or large as a cow;
But my old lad Tim he'll never be bet
By any dog that ever he met.
'Come on,' says he, 'for I'm not kilt yet.'

No matter the size of the dog he'll meet,
Tim trails his coat the length o' the street.
D'ye mind his scars an' his ragged ear,
The like of a Dublin Fusilier?
He's a massacree dog that knows no fear.

But he'd stick to me till his latest breath;
An' he'd go with me to the gates of death.
He'd wait for a thousand years, maybe,
Scratching the door an' whining for me
If myself were inside Purgatory.

So I laugh when I hear thim make it plain
That dogs and men never meet again.

[116]

For all their talk who'd listen to thim,
With the soul in the shining eyes of him?
Would God be wasting a dog like Tim?

Why the Cats Wash After Eating

You may have noticed, little friends,
    That cats don't wash their faces
Before they eat, as children do,
    In all good Christian places.

Well, years ago a famous cat,
    The pangs of hunger feeling,
Had chanced to catch a fine young mouse,
    Who said, as he ceased squealing:

'All genteel folks their faces wash
    Before they think of eating!'
And, wishing to be thought well bred,
    Puss heeded his entreating.

But when she raised her paw to wash,
    Chance for escape affording,
The sly young mouse said his good-bye,
    Without respect to wording.

A feline council met that day,
    And passed, in solemn meeting,
A law, forbidding any cat
    To wash till after eating.

ANONYMOUS

June

Now summer is in flower, and Nature's hum
Is never silent round her bounteous bloom;
Insects, as small as dust, have never done

[117]

With glitt'ring dance, and reeling in the sun;
And green wood-fly, and blossom-haunting bee,
Are never weary of their melody.
Round field and hedge, flowers in full glory twine,
Large bindweed bells, wild hop, and streak'd woodbine,
That lift athirst their slender-throated flowers,
Agape for dew-falls, and for honey showers;
These o'er each bush in sweet disorder run,
And spread their wild hues to the sultry sun.
The mottled spider, at eve's leisure, weaves
His webs of silken lace on twigs and leaves,
Which every morning meet the poet's eye,
Like fairies' dew-wet dresses hung to dry.

JOHN CLARE. 1793-1864

HUMOUR

Lying

I do confess, in many a sigh,
   My lips have breathed you many a lie;
And who, with such delights in view,
Would lose them, for a lie or two?

Nay,—look not thus, with brow reproving,
Lies are, my dear, the soul of loving;
If half we tell the girls were true,
If half we swear to think and do,
Were aught but lying's bright illusion,
This world would be in strange confusion.
If ladies' eyes were, every one,

As lovers swear, a radiant sun,
Astronomy must leave the skies,
To learn her lore in ladies' eyes.
Oh no—believe me, lovely girl,
When nature turns your teeth to pearl,
Your neck to snow, your eyes to fire,
Your amber locks to golden wire,
Then, only then can Heaven decree,
That you should live for only me,
Or I for you, as night and morn,
We've swearing kist, and kissing sworn.
And now, my gentle hints to clear,
For once I'll tell you truth, my dear.
Whenever you may chance to meet
Some loving youth whose love is sweet,
Long as you're false and he believes you,
Long as you trust and he deceives you,
So long the blissful bond endures,
And while he lies, his heart is yours:
But oh! you've wholly lost the youth
The instant that he tells you truth.

THOMAS MOORE. 1779–1852

Drinking

The thirsty earth soaks up the rain,
And drinks and gapes for drink again;
The plants suck in the earth, and are
With constant drinking fresh and fair;
The sea itself (which one would think
Should have but little need of drink)
Drinks twice ten thousand rivers up,
So fill'd that they o'erflow the cup.
The busy sun (and one would guess
By's drunken fiery face no less)
Drinks up the sea, and when he's done,
The Moon and Stars drink up the Sun:
They drink and dance by their own light,
They drink and revel all the night:
Nothing in Nature's sober found,
But an eternal health goes round.
Fill up the bowl, then, fill it high,
Fill all the glasses there—for why
Should every creature drink but I?
Why, Man of Morals, tell me why?

ABRAHAM COWLEY. 1618–1677

The Country Squire

In a small pretty village in Nottinghamshire,
There formerly lived a respectable Squire,
Who excelled all his friends in amusements athletic,
And whose manner of living was far from ascetic.

A wife he had taken for better for worse,
Whose temper had proved an intolerant curse;
But at length, to his great and unspeakable joy,
She dies when presenting a fine little boy.

Strange fancies men have! the father designed
To watch o'er the dawn of his son's youthful mind—
That, only approached by the masculine gender,
No room should be left him for feelings more tender.

'Had I ne'er seen a woman,' he often would sigh,
'What squire in the country so happy as I!'

The boy was intelligent, active, and bright,
And took in his studies uncommon delight;
No juvenile follies distracted his mind—
No visions of bright eyes or damsels unkind;

And those fair demi-sisterly beings so gay,
Yclept 'pretty cousins,' ne'er popped in his way:
Till at length this remarkably singular son
Could number of years that had passed twenty-one.

Now the father had settled, his promising son
Should his studies conclude when he reached twenty-one:
And he went with a heart beating high with emotion,
To launch the young man on life's turbulent ocean.

As they entered the town, a young maiden tripped by,
With a cheek like a rose, and a light laughing eye.
'Oh! father, what's that?' cried the youth with delight,
As this vision of loveliness burst on his sight.

'Oh that,' cried the cautious and politic Squire,
Who did not the youth's ardent glances admire,
Is only a thing called a Goose, my dear son—
We shall see many more ere our visit is done.'

Blooming damsels now passed with their butter and cheese,
Whose beauty might even an anchorite please:
'Merely geese!' said the Squire: 'don't mind them, my dear;
There are many things better worth looking at here.'

As onward they passed, every step brought to view
Some spectacle equally curious and new;
And the joy of the youth hardly knew any bounds
At the rope-dancers, tumblers, and merry-go-rounds.

[123]

And soon, when the tour of the town was completed,
The father resolved that the boy should be treated;
So, pausing an instant he said, 'My dear son,
A new era to-day in your life has begun:

Now of all this bright scene and the gaieties in it,
Choose whatever you like—it is yours from this minute.'
'Choose whatever I like?' cried the youthful recluse;
'O thank you, dear father, then give me a goose!'

BENTLEY BALLADS

Elegy on the Death of a Mad Dog

Good people all, of every sort,
　　Give ear unto my Song;
And if you find it wond'rous short,
　　It cannot hold you long.

In Isling town there was a man,
　　Of whom the world might say,
That still a godly race he ran,
　　When'er he went to pray.

A kind and gentle heart he had,
　　To comfort friends and foes;
The naked every day he clad,
　　When he put on his clothes.

And in that town a dog was found,
　　As many dogs there be,
Both mungrel, puppy, whelp and hound,
　　And curs of low degree.

The dog and man at first were friends;
　　But when a pique began,
The dog, to gain his private ends,
　　Went mad and bit the man.

[124]

Around from all the neighbouring streets,
    The wondering neighbours ran,
And swore the dog had lost his wits,
    To bite so good a man.

The wound it seem'd both sore and sad,
    To every christian eye;
And while they swore the dog was mad,
    They swore the man would die.

But soon a wonder came to light,
    That shew'd the rogues they lied,
The man recovered of the bite,
    The dog it was that dy'd.

OLIVER GOLDSMITH. 1728–1774

Catching the Cat

The mice had met in council,
    They all looked haggard and worn,
For the state of affairs was too terrible
    To be any longer borne.
Not a family out of mourning,—
    There was crape on every hat,—
They were desperate—something must be done
    And done at once, to the cat.

Then rather an old mouse rose, and said:
    'It might prove a possible thing
To set the trap which they set for us—
    That one with the awful spring!'
The suggestion was applauded
    Loudly by one and all,
Till somebody squeaked: 'That trap would be
    About ninety-five times too small!'

Then a medical mouse suggested
    (A little under his breath):
'If you confiscate the very first mouse
    That dies a natural death,

I'll undertake to poison the cat,
  If you'll let me prepare that mouse.'
'There's not been a natural death,' they shrieked,
  'Since the cat came into the house!'

The smallest mouse in the council
  Arose with a solemn air,
And, by way of increasing his stature,
  Rubbed up his whiskers and hair.
He waited until there was silence
  All along the pantry shelf,
And then he said with dignity,
  'I will catch the cat myself!

'When next I hear her coming,
  Instead of running away,
I shall turn and face her boldly,
  And pretend to be at play.
She will not see her danger,
  Poor creature! I suppose;
But as she stoops to catch me,
  I shall catch her, by the nose!'

The mice began to look hopeful,
  Yes, even the old ones, when
A grey-haired mouse said slowly,
  'And what will you do with her then?'
The champion disconcerted,
  Replied with dignity, 'Well—
I think, if you'll excuse me,
  'Twould be wiser not to tell!

'We all have our inspirations,'—
  This produced a general smirk,—
'But we are not all at liberty
  To explain just how they'll work.
I ask you simply to trust me;
  You need have no further fears—
Consider our enemy done for!'
  The council gave three cheers.

'I do believe she's coming!'
    Said a small mouse nervously.
'Run if you like,' said the champion,
    'But I shall wait and see!'
And sure enough she was coming—
    The mice all scampered away,
Except the noble champion,
    Who had made up his mind to stay.

The mice had faith,—of course they had,
    They were all of them trusting souls,—
But a sort of general feeling
    Kept them safely in their holes,
Until sometime in the evening;
    Then the boldest ventured out,
And there he saw in the distance
    The cat prance gaily about!

There was dreadful consternation,
    Till some one at last said, 'Oh,
He's not had time to do it,
    Let us not prejudge him so!'
'I believe in him, of course I do,'
    Said the nervous mouse with a sigh,
'But the cat looks uncommonly happy,
    And I wish I did know why!'

The cat, I regret to mention,
    Still prances about that house,
And no message, letter, or telegram
    Has come from the champion mouse.
The mice are a little discouraged;
    The demand for crape goes on;
They feel they'd be happier if they knew
    Where the champion mouse has gone.

This story has a moral,—
    It is very short you'll see,—
So, of course, you all will listen,
    For fear of offending me.

It is well to be courageous,
  And valiant, and all that,
But—if you are mice—you'd better think twice,
  Before you catch the cat.

MARGARET VANDERGRIFT JANVIER

The Twins

In form and feature, face and limb,
  I grew so like my brother,
That folks got taking me for him,
  And each for one another.
It puzzled all our kith and kin,
  It reached a fearful pitch;
For one of us was born a twin,
  And not a soul knew which.

One day to make the matter worse,
  Before our names were fixed,
As we were being washed by nurse,
  We got completely mixed;
And thus, you see, by Fate's decree,
  Or rather nurse's whim,
My brother John got christened me,
  And I got christened him.

This fatal likeness ever dogged
  My footsteps when at school,
And I was always getting flogged,
  When John turned out a fool.
I put this question, fruitlessly,
  To everyone I knew:
'What would you do, if you were me,
  To prove that you were you?'

Our close resemblance turned the tide
  Of my domestic life,
For somehow, my intended bride
  Became my brother's wife.

In fact, year after year the same
        Absurd mistakes went on,
And when I died, the neighbours came
        And buried brother John.

HENRY S. LEIGH

Kitty of Coleraine

As beautiful Kitty one morning was trippin'
        With a pitcher of milk from the fair of Coleraine,
When she saw me she stumbled, the pitcher down tumbled,
        And all the sweet butther-milk wathered the plain.
'Oh! what shall I do now? 'twas looking at you, now;
        Sure, sure, such a pitcher I'll ne'er meet again;
'Twas the pride of my dairy! O Barney M'Cleary,
        You're sent as a plague to the girls of Coleraine!'

I sat down beside her, and gently did chide her,
        That so small a misfortune should give her such pain;
A kiss then I gave her, and, ere I did lave her,
        She vowed for such pleasure she'd break it again.
'Twas hay-making sayson—I can't tell the rayson—
        Misfortunes 'ill never come single, 'tis plain;
For very soon after poor Kitty's disaster
        The divil a pitcher was whole in Coleraine.

ANONYMOUS

Widow Malone

    Did you hear of the Widow Malone,
                Ohone!
    Who lived in the town of Athlone,
                Alone!
        Oh, she melted the hearts
        Of the swains in them parts:
    So lovely the Widow Malone,
                Ohone!
    So lovely the Widow Malone.

Of lovers she had a full score,
        Or more;
And fortunes they all had galore,
        In store.
    From minister down
    To the clerk of the Crown,
All were courting the Widow Malone,
        Ohone!
All were courting the Widow Malone.

But so modest was Mistress Malone,
        'Twas known
That no one could see her alone,
        Ohone!
    Let them ogle and sigh,
    They could ne'er catch her eye
So bashful the Widow Malone,
        Ohone!
So bashful the Widow Malone.

Till one Misther O'Brien, from Clare,
        (How quare!
It's little for blushing they care
        Down there),
    Put his arm round her waist,
    Gave ten kisses at laste,
'Oh,' says he, 'you're my Molly Malone,
        My own!
Oh,' says he, 'you're my Molly Malone!'

And the widow they all thought so shy,
        My eye!
Ne'er thought of a simper or sigh,—
        For why?
    But, 'Lucius,' says she,
    'Since you've now made so free,
You may marry your Mary Malone,
        Ohone!
You may marry your Mary Malone.'

There's a moral contained in my song
                    Not wrong;
And one comfort, it's not very long,
                    But strong,—
        If for widows you die,
        Learn to kiss, not to sigh;
For they're all like sweet Mistress Malone,
                    Ohone!
Oh, they're all like sweet Mistress Malone!

CHARLES LEVER. 1809–1872

Nonsense

Good reader! if you e'er have seen,
        When Phœbus hastens to his pillow,
The mermaids, with their tresses green,
        Dancing upon the western billow:
If you have seen, at twilight dim,
When the lone spirit's vesper hymn
        Floats wild along the winding shore
If you have seen, through mist of eve,
The fairy train their ringlets weave,
Glancing along the spangled green;—
        If you have seen all this, and more,
God bless me! what a deal you've seen.

THOMAS MOORE. 1779–1852

The Sorrows of Werther

Werther had a love for Charlotte
        Such as words could never utter;
Would you know how first he met her?
        She was cutting bread and butter.

Charlotte was a married lady,
        And a moral man was Werther,

And for all the wealth of Indies,
      Would do nothing for to hurt her.

So he sigh'd and pined and ogled,
      And his passion boil'd and bubbled,
Till he blew his silly brains out,
      And no more was by it troubled.

Charlotte, having seen his body
      Borne before her on a shutter,
Like a well-conducted person,
      Went on cutting bread and butter.

W. M. THACKERAY. 1811–1863

The Hindu's Paradise

A Hindu died—a happy thing to do
When twenty years united to a shrew.
Released, he hopefully for entrance cries
Before the gates of Brahma's paradise.
'Hast been through purgatory?' Brahma said.
'I have been married'—and he hung his head.
'Come in, come in, and welcome, too, my son
Marriage and purgatory are as one.'
In bliss extreme he entered heaven's door,
And knew the peace he ne'er had known before.

Scarce had he entered on that garden fair,
Another Hindu asked admission there.
The self-same question Brahma asked again:
'Hast been through purgatory?' 'No—what then?
'Thou canst not enter!' did the god reply.
'He who went in has been no more than I.'
'All that is true, but he has married been,
And so on earth has suffered for his sin!'

[132]

'Married? 'Tis well; for I've been married twice!'
'Begone! We'll have no fools in Paradise!'

The Curate's Kindness

I thought they'd be strangers aroun' me,
    But she's to be there!
Let me jump out o' waggon and go back and drown me
    At Pummery or Ten-Hatches Weir.

I thought: 'Well, I've come to the Union—
    The workhouse at last—
After honest hard work all the week, and Communion
    O' Zundays, these fifty years past.

'Tis hard; but,' I thoughtm 'never mind it:
    There's gain in the end:
And when I get used to the place I shall find it
    A home, and may find there a friend.

'Life there will be better than t'other,
    For peace is assured.
The men in one wing and their wives in another
    Is strictly the rule of the Board.'

Just then one young Pa'son arriving
    Steps up out of breath
To the side o' the waggon wherein we were driving
    To Union; and calls out and saith:

'Old folks, that harsh order is altered,
    Be not sick of heart!
The Guardians they poohed and they pished and they paltered
    When urged not to keep you apart.

'"It is wrong," I maintained, "to divide them,
    Near forty years wed."

[133]

"Very well, sir. We promise, then, they shall abide them
   In one wing together," they said.'

Then I sank—knew 'twas quite a foredone thing
   That misery should be
To the end! . . . To get freed of her there was the one thing
   Had made the change welcome to me.

To go there was ending but badly;
   'Twas shame and 'twas pain;
'But anyhow,' thought I, 'thereby I shall gladly
   Get free of this forty years' chain.'

I thought they'd be strangers aroun' me,
   But she's to be there!
Let me jump out o' waggon and go back and drown me
   At Pummery or Ten-Hatches Weir.

THOMAS HARDY. 1840–1928

The Well of St. Keyne

A well there is in the west country,
   And a clearer one never was seen;
There is not a wife in the west country
   But has heard of the Well of St. Keyne.

An oak and an elm tree stand beside,
   And behind doth an ash-tree grow,
And a willow from the bank above
   Droops to the water below.

A traveller came to the Well of St. Keyne;
   Joyfully he drew nigh;
For from cock-crow he had been travelling,
   And there was not a cloud in the sky.

[134]

He drank of the water so cool and clear,
 For thirsty and hot was he,
And he sat down upon the bank,
 Under the willow-tree.

There came a man from the house hard by,
 At the Well to fill his pail,
On the Well-side he rested it,
 And bade the Stranger hail.

'Now, art thou a bachelor, Stranger?' quoth he,
 'For, an if thou hast a wife,
The happiest draught thou hast drank this day
 That ever thou didst in thy life.

'Or has thy good woman, if one thou hast,
 Ever here in Cornwall been?
For, an if she have, I'll venture my life
 She has drunk from the Well of St. Keyne.'

'I have left a good woman who never was here,'
 The Stranger he made reply;
'But that my draught should be better for that,
 I pray you answer me why.'

'St. Keyne,' quoth the Cornish-man, 'many a time
 Drank from the crystal Well;
And, before the angel summoned her,
 She laid on the water a spell,—

'If the Husband, of this gifted Well
 Shall drink before his Wife,
A happy man henceforth is he,
 For he shall be Master for life;—

'But, if the Wife should drink of it first,
 Heaven help the Husband then!'—
The Stranger stooped to the Well of St. Keyne,
 And drank of the water again.

[135]

'You drank of the Well, I warrant, betimes?'
    He to the Cornish-man said;
But the Cornish-man smiled as the Stranger spake,
    And sheepishly shook his head:—

'I hastened, as soon as the wedding was done,
    And left my Wife in the porch;
But i' faith, she had been wiser than me,
    For she took a bottle to church.'

ROBERT SOUTHEY. 1774–1843

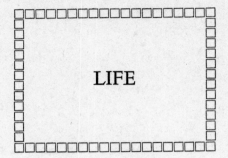

LIFE

Song

Go and catch a falling star,
    Get with child a mandrake root,
Tell me where all past years are,
    Or who cleft the Devil's foot;
Teach me to hear mermaids singing,
Or to keep off envy's stinging,
        And find
        What wind
Serves to advance an honest mind.

If thou be'st born to strange sights,
    Things invisible to see,
Ride ten thousand days and nights
    Till Age snow white hairs on thee;
Thou, when thou return'st, wilt tell me
All strange wonders that befell thee,
        And swear
        No where
Lives a woman true and fair.

If thou find'st one, let me know;
    Such a pilgrimage were sweet.
Yet do not; I would not go,
    Though at next door we might meet.
Though she were true when you met her,
And last till you write your letter,
        Yet she
        Will be
False, ere I come, to two or three.

JOHN DONNE. 1573–1631

Wensleydale Lullaby

Settle doon, my Poppet joy,
Noo t'birds an' t'beasts are sleepin',
Settle doon, my bonnie boy,

T'breet stars ther watch are keepin';
When thoo wakes, I'll gie to thee
Money things for laikin'*
'At thoo will rejoice to see
An' can have for takin';
Two black lambkins, muther-lorn,
A white an' ginger kitten,
A puppy 'at is newly born,
A 'broidered chair to sit on,
Thoo shall have a dappled foal
An' a leaf-green cart,
Honey in a sky-blue bowl,
My sweetin', my sweetheart!
Cuddle doon an' close thine eyes
Noo t'birds an' t'beasts are sleepin',
Cuddle doon, my luvely doy,†
T'Lord ha'e thee in His keepin'.

DOROTHY UNA RATCLIFFE

The Toys

My little Son, who look'd from thoughtful eyes
    And moved and spoke in quiet grown-up wise,
Having my law the seventh time disobey'd,
I struck him, and dismiss'd
With hard words and unkiss'd,
—His Mother, who was patient, being dead.
Then, fearing lest his grief should hinder sleep,
I visited his bed,
But found him slumbering deep,
With darken'd eyelids, and their lashes yet
From his late sobbing wet.
And I, with moan,
Kissing away his tears, left others of my own;
For, on a table drawn beside his head,
He had put, within his reach,
A box of counters and a red-vein'd stone,

* To play with.   † Darling.

[140]

A piece of glass abraded by the beach,
And six or seven shells,
A bottle with bluebells,
And two French copper coins, ranged there with careful art,
To comfort his sad heart.
So when that night I pray'd
To God, I wept, and said:
Ah, when at last we lie with tranced breath,
Not vexing Thee in death,
And Thou rememberest of what toys
We made our joys,
How weakly understood
Thy great commanded good,
Then, fatherly not less
Than I whom Thou hast moulded from the clay,
Thou'lt leave Thy wrath, and say.
'I will be sorry for their childishness.'

COVENTRY PATMORE. 1823–1896

The Village Parson

. . . Near yonder copse, where once the garden smiled,
And still where many a garden flower grows wild;
There, where a few torn shrubs the place disclose,
The village preacher's modest mansion rose.
A man he was, to all the country dear,
And passing rich with forty pounds a year;
Remote from towns he ran his godly race,
Nor e'er had changed, nor wished to change his place;
Unpractised he to fawn, or seek for power,
By doctrines fashioned to the varying hour;
Far other aims his heart had learned to prize,
More skilled to raise the wretched than to rise.
His house was known to all the vagrant train,
He chid their wanderings, but relieved their pain;
The long remembered beggar was his guest,
Whose beard descending swept his aged breast;
The ruined spendthrift, now no longer proud,

Claimed kindred there, and had his claims allowed;
The broken soldier, kindly bade to stay,
Sate by his fire, and talked the night away;
Wept o'er his wounds, or tales of sorrow done,
Shouldered his crutch, and shewed how fields were won.
Pleased with his guests, the good man learned to glow,
And quite forgot their vices in their woe;
Careless their merits, or their faults to scan,
His pity gave ere charity began.

  Thus to relieve the wretched was his pride,
And even his failings leaned to Virtue's side;
But in his duty prompt at every call,
He watched and wept, he prayed and felt, for all.
And, as a bird each fond endearment tries,
To tempt its new fledged offspring to the skies;
He tried each art, reproved each dull delay,
Allured to brighter worlds, and led the way.

  Beside the bed where parting life was laid,
And sorrow, guilt, and pain, by turns dismayed
The reverend champion stood. At his control,
Despair and anguish fled the struggling soul;
Comfort came down the trembling wretch to raise,
And his last faltering accents whispered praise.

  At church, with meek and unaffected grace,
His looks adorned the venerable place;
Truth from his lips prevailed with double sway,
And fools, who came to scoff, remained to pray.
The service past, around the pious man,
With steady zeal each honest rustic ran;
Even children followed with endearing wile,
And plucked his gown, to share the good man's smile.
His ready smile a parent's warmth exprest,
Their welfare pleased him, and their cares distrest;
To them his heart, his love, his griefs were given,
But all his serious thoughts had rest in Heaven.
As some tall cliff that lifts its awful form,
Swells from the vale, and midway leaves the storm,
Tho' round its breast the rolling clouds are spread,
Eternal sunshine settles on its head . . .

OLIVER GOLDSMITH. 1728–1774

[142]

A Gradely Prayer

Give us, Lord,
    A bit o' sun,
A bit o' wark,
    An' a bit o' fun,
Give us aw
    In th' struggle an' splutter,
Eaur daily bread—
    An' a bit o' butter.

Give us health,
    Eaur keep to make,
An' a bit to spare
    For poor folk's sake;
Give us sense,
    For we're some of us duffers,
An' a heart to feel
    For them that suffers.

Give us, too,
    A bit of a song,
An' a tale an' a book
    To help us along;
An' give us eaur share
    O' sorrow's lesson
That we may prove
    Heaw grief's a blessin'

Give us, Lord,
    A chance to be
Eaur gradely best,
    Brave, wise, an' free;
Eaur gradely best
    For eaursels an' others,
Till all men larn
    To live as brothers.

ALLEN CLARKE

Lookin' Back

When t'lamp's aleet at t'top o' t' street
An' t' fooaks are comin' whoam at neet,
An' t' wark's o' done an' t' childer still
An' t' moon's aflooat at back o' t' hill—
Ah like to ceawr bi t'fire misen,
Id o' comes back soa plainly then
(Though thirty-odd years lie between)
Thad Wakes when Ah wor seventeen!

We'd saved a bit o' brass tha knows,
Young Mary-Jane an' me an' Rose—
An' oaf we seet, as preawd as Punch
To be on' t' booat an' hevin' lunch!
Runs i' mi yead thad summer day,
Heaw green an' gowd th' owd Island lay
Wi summat o'er id like a sheen—
Thad Wakes when Ah wor seventeen!

Well, t' chaps come mashin' t' other two,
But me—Ah'd fun eawt summat new,
An Island lad fro' t' fishin' fleet—
Heaw daft id wor! Heaw sad! Heaw sweet!
Id's o' mixed up, his lazy smiles
An' t' way he reyched me ower t' stiles,
Wi fuschsia fleawrs he creawned me Queen,
Thad Wakes when Ah wor seventeen!

An' neaw Ah shift as weel Ah con
Wi' t' childer an' a crabby mon!
But sometimes, when Ah'm stitchin' at
Eawr Billy's pants, Eawr Sally's brat,*
Ah stop—an' think o' t' way we went
An' wod thad breawn lad's kisses meant.
Eh, an' them loines!—their gowd an' green!
Thad Wakes when Ah wor seventeen.

* brat – apron

[144]

A lot o' watter's gone id way
Sin Ah wor young an' pert an' gay,
Sin t' sky wor dazzlin' blue aboon
An' Ah went walkin' under t' moon.
We goa for t'Wakes to Blackpoo' neaw—
But thad corn'd stop me thinkin' heaw
An Island bed a silver sheen
Thad Wakes when Ah wor seventeen!

JOAN POMFRET

Pendle Nestlin' Song

Cock-a-loo, a-laddie, O
Just thee howd thi hush an' O;
Fer t'neet has lapped id shawl areawned
Owd Pendle's grey-blue hill.
Soa, sniggle to thi mammy, O
Mi cock-a-loo, a-laddie, O;
An' rest thee quate like t' craathurs do,
When t' daark bids 'em be still!

Cock-a-loo, a-laddie, O
Just thee shut thi een, an' O;
Fer up an' deawn the siller steeors
Owd Nod ull ride a' neet:
He weeors, he weeors green buckles, O
Mi cock-a-loo, a-laddie, O;
An' t' moon ull paint a' t' winda panes,
Till mornin' brings cock-leet!

Cock-a-loo, a-laddie, O,
Just thee goa to sleep, an' O;
Fer sleepin' time is growin' time
Fer t' chuckies, an' fer thee!
Soa dunna laik abeawt so much;
A-showin' a' thi chaarms, an' such—
Mi cock-a-loo, a-laddie, ay,
Mi cock-a-loo, a-lee!

ALICE MILLER

The Arrest of Oscar Wilde at the Cadogan Hotel

He sipped at a weak hock and seltzer
    As he gazed at the London skies
Through the Nottingham lace of the curtains
    Or was it his bees-winged eyes?

To the right and before him Pont Street
    Did tower in her new built red,
As hard as the morning gaslight
    That shone on his unmade bed,

'I want some more hock in my seltzer,
    And Robbie, please give me your hand—
Is this the end or beginning?
    How can I understand?

'So you've brought me the latest Yellow Book:
    And Buchan has got in it now:
Approval of what is approved of
    Is as false as a well-kept vow.

'More hock, Robbie—where is the seltzer?
    Dear boy, pull again at the bell!
They are all little better than cretins,
    Though this is the Cadogan Hotel.

'One astrakhan coat is at Willis's—
    Another one's at the Savoy:
Do fetch my morocco portmanteau,
    And bring them on later, dear boy.'

A thump, and a murmur of voices—
    ('Oh why must they make such a din?')
As the door of the bedroom swung open
    And TWO PLAIN CLOTHES POLICEMEN came in:

'Mr. Woilde, we 'ave come for tew take yew
    Where felons and criminals dwell:

We must ask yew tew leave with us quoietly
    For this is the Cadogan Hotel.'

He rose, and he put down the Yellow Book.
    He staggered—and, terrible-eyed,
He brushed past the palms on the staircase
    And was helped to a hansom outside.

JOHN BETJEMAN

The Hound of Heaven

I fled Him, down the nights and down the days;
    I fled Him, down the arches of the years;
    I fled Him, down the labyrinthine ways
Of my own mind; and in the mist of tears
I hid from Him, and under running laughter.
            Up vistaed hopes I sped;
            And shot, precipitated,
Adown Titanic glooms of chasmed fears,
    From those strong Feet that followed, followed after.
            But with unhurrying chase,
            And unperturbed pace,
    Deliberate speed, majestic instancy,
            They beat—and a Voice beat
            More instant than the Feet—
'All things betray thee, who betrayest Me.'

            I pleaded, outlaw-wise,
By many a hearted casement, curtained red,
    Trellised with intertwining charities;
(For, though I knew His love Who followed,
            Yet was I sore adread
Lest, having Him, I must have naught beside.)
But, if one little casement parted wide,
    The gust of His approach would clash it to:
    Fear wist not to evade, as Love wist to pursue.
Across the margent of the world I fled,
    And troubled the gold gateways of the stars,

[147]

Smiting for shelter on their clanged bars;
          Fretted to dulcet jars
And silvern chatter the pale ports o' the moon.
I said to Dawn: Be sudden—to Eve: Be soon;
     With thy young skiey blossoms heap me over
          From this tremendous Lover—
Float thy vague veil about me, lest He see!
     I tempted all His servitors, but to find
My own betrayal in their constancy,
In faith to Him their fickleness to me,
     Their traitorous trueness, and their loyal deceit.
To all swift things for swiftness did I sue;
     Clung to the whistling mane of every wind.

          But whether they swept, smoothly fleet,
     The long savannahs of the blue;
          Or whether, Thunder-driven,
          They clanged his chariot 'thwart a heaven,
Plashy with flying lightnings round the spurn o' their feet:—
Fear wist not to evade as Love wist to pursue.
          Still with unhurrying chase,
          And unperturbed pace,
     Deliberate speed, majestic instancy,
          Came on the following Feet,
          And a Voice above their beat—
     'Naught shelters thee, who wilt not shelter Me.'

I sought no more that after which I strayed
          In face of man or maid;
But still within the little children's eyes
          Seems something, something that replies,
They at least are for me, surely for me!
I turned me to them very wistfully;
But just as their young eyes grew sudden fair
          With dawning answers there,
Their angel plucked them from me by the hair.
'Come then, ye other children, Nature's—share
With me' (said I) 'your delicate fellowship;
          Let me greet you lip to lip,
          Let me twine with you caresses,
               Wantoning

With our Lady-Mother's vagrant tresses,
   Banqueting
With her in her wind-walled palace,
Underneath her azured dais,
Quaffing, as your taintless way is,
   From a chalice
Lucent-weeping out of the dayspring.'
   So it was done:
I in their delicate fellowship was one—
Drew the bolt of Nature's secrecies.
   I knew all the swift importings
   On the wilful face of skies;
   I knew how the clouds arise
   Spumed of the wild sea-snortings;
   All that's born or dies
   Rose and drooped with; made them shapers
Of mine own moods, or wailful or divine;
   With them joyed and was bereaven.
   I was heavy with the even,
   When she lit her glimmering tapers
   Round the day's dead sanctities.
   I laughed in the morning's eyes.
I triumphed and I saddened with all weather,
   Heaven and I wept together,
And its sweet tears were salt with mortal mine;
Against the red throb of its sunset-heart
   I laid my own to beat,
   And share commingling heat;
But not by that, by that, was eased my human smart.
In vain my tears were wet on Heaven's grey cheek.
For ah! we know not what each other says,
   These things and I; in sound I speak—
Their sound is but their stir, they speak by silences.
Nature, poor stepdame, cannot slake my drouth;
   Let her, if she would owe me,
Drop yon blue bosom-veil of sky, and show me
   The breasts o' her tenderness:
Never did any milk of hers once bless
   My thirsting mouth.
   Nigh and nigh draws the chase,

With unperturbed pace,
Deliberate speed, majestic instancy;
And past those noised Feet
A voice comes yet more fleet—
'Lo! naught contents thee, who content'st not Me.'

Naked I wait Thy love's uplifted stroke!
My harness piece by piece Thou hast hewn from me,
And smitten me to my knee;
I am defenceless utterly.
I slept, methinks, and woke,
And, slowly gazing, find me stripped in sleep.
In the rash lustihead of my young powers,
I shook the pillaring hours
And pulled my life upon me; grimed with smears,
I stand amid the dust o' the mounded years—
My mangled youth lies dead beneath the heap.
My days have crackled and gone up in smoke,
Have puffed and burst as sun-starts on a stream.
Yea, faileth now even dream
The dreamer, and the lute the lutanist;
Even the linked fantasies, in whose blossomy twist
I swung the earth a trinket at my wrist,
Are yielding; cords of all too weak account
For earth with heavy griefs so overplussed.
Ah! is Thy love indeed
A weed, albeit an amaranthine weed,
Suffering no flowers except its own to mount?
Ah! must—
Designer infinite!—
Ah! must Thou char the wood ere Thou canst limn with it?
My freshness spent its wavering shower i' the dust;
And now my heart is as a broken fount,
Wherein tear-drippings stagnate, spilt down ever
From the dank thoughts that shiver
Upon the sighful branches of my mind.
Such is; what is to be?
The pulp so bitter, how shall taste the rind?
I dimly guess what Time in mists confounds;
Yet ever and anon a trumpet sounds

From the hid battlements of Eternity;
Those shaken mists a space unsettle, then
Round the half-glimpsed turrets slowly wash again.
        But not ere him who summoneth
        I first have seen, enwound
With glooming robes purpureal, cypress-crowned;
His name I know, and what his trumpet saith.
Whether man's heart or life it be which yields
        Thee harvest, must Thy harvest-fields
        Be dunged with rotten death?

        Now of that long pursuit
        Comes on at hand the bruit;
    That Voice is round me like a bursting sea:
        'And is thy earth so marred,
        Shattered in shard on shard?
    Lo, all things fly thee, for thou fliest Me!
        Strange, piteous, futile thing!
Wherefore should any set thee love apart?
Seeing none but I makes much of naught' (He said),
'And human love needs human meriting:
        How hast thou merited—
Of all man's clotted clay the dingiest clot?
        Alack, thou knowest not
How little worthy of any love thou art!
Whom wilt thou find to love ignoble thee,
        Save Me, save only Me?
All which I took from thee I did but take,
        Not for thy harms,
But just that thou might'st seek it in My arms.
        All which thy child's mistake
Fancies as lost, I have stored for thee at home:
        Rise, clasp My hand, and come!'
    Halts by me that footfall:
    Is my gloom, after all,
Shade of His hand, outstretched caressingly?
    'Ah, fondest, blindest, weakest,
    I am He Whom thou seekest!
Thou dravest love from thee, who dravest Me.'

FRANCIS THOMPSON. 1859–1907

'Les Sylphides'

Life in a day: he took his girl to the ballet;
Being shortsighted himself could hardly see it—
      The white skirts in the grey
      Glade and the swell of the music
      Lifting the white sails.

Calyx upon calyx, canterbury bells in the breeze
The flowers on the left mirror to the flowers on the right
      And the naked arms above—
      The powdered faces moving
      Like seaweed in a pool.

Now, he thought, we are floating—ageless, oarless—
Now there is no separation, from now on—
      You will be wearing white—
      Satin and a red sash
      Under the waltzing trees.

But the music stopped, the dancers took their curtain,
The river had come to a lock—a shuffle of programmes—
      And we cannot continue down
      Stream unless we are ready—
      To enter the lock and drop.

So they were married—to be the more together—
And found they were never again so much together,
      Divided by the morning tea,
      By the evening paper,
      By children and tradesman's bills.

Waking at times in the night she found assurance—
In his regular breathing but wondered whether
      It was really worth it and where
      The river had flowed away
      And where were the white flowers.

LOUIS MACNEICE

Mother Wept

Mother wept, and father sigh'd;
  With delight aglow
Cried the lad, 'To-morrow', cried,
  'To the pit I go.'

Up and down the place he sped,—
  Greeted old and young;
Far and wide the tidings spread;
  Clapt his hands and sung.

Came his cronies; some to gaze
  Wrapp'd in wonder; some
Free with counsel; some with praise;
  Some with envy dumb.

'May he,' many a gossip cried,
  'Be from peril kept.'
Father hid his face and sigh'd,
  Mother turn'd and wept.

JOSEPH SKIPSEY

Peace

My soul, there is a country
  Far beyond the stars,
Where stands a winged sentry
  All skilful in the wars:
There, above noise and danger,
  Sweet Peace sits crown'd with smiles,
And One born in a manger
  Commands the beauteous files.
He is thy gracious Friend,
  And—O my soul, awake!—
Did in pure love descend

[153]

To die here for thy sake.
If thou canst get but thither,
There grows the flower of Peace,
The Rose that cannot wither,
Thy fortress, and thy ease.
Leave then thy foolish ranges;
For none can thee secure
But One who never changes—
Thy God, thy life, thy cure.

HENRY VAUGHAN. 1621–1695

The Shepherd Boy Sings in the Valley of Humiliation

He that is down needs fear no fall,
He that is low, no pride;
He that is humble ever shall
Have God to be his guide.

I am content with what I have,
Little be it or much:
And, Lord, contentment still I crave,
Because Thou savest such.

Fullness to such a burden is
That go on pilgrimage:
Here little, and hereafter bliss,
Is best from age to age.

JOHN BUNYAN. 1628–1688

Part of Intimations of Immortality from Recollections of Early Childhood

There was a time when meadow, grove, and stream,
The earth, and every common sight,
To me did seem
Apparell'd in celestial light,

The glory and the freshness of a dream.
It is not now as it hath been of yore;—
      Turn wheresoe'er I may,
            By night or day,
The things which I have seen I now can see no more.

        The rainbow comes and goes,
        And lovely is the rose;
        The moon doth with delight
Look round her when the heavens are bare;
        Waters on a starry night
        Are beautiful and fair;
      The sunshine is a glorious birth;
      But yet I know, where'er I go,
That there hath pass'd away a glory from the earth.

Now, while the birds thus sing a joyous song,
      And while the young lambs bound
        As to the tabor's sound,
To me alone there came a thought of grief:
A timely utterance gave that thought relief,
        And I again am strong:
The cataracts blow their trumpets from the steep;
No more shall grief of mine the season wrong;
I hear the echoes through the mountains throng,
The winds come to me from the fields of sleep,

      And all the earth is gay;
        Land and sea
Give themselves up to jollity,
      And with the heart of May
Doth every beast keep holiday;—
        Thou Child of Joy,
Shout round me, let me hear thy shouts, thou happy
        Shepherd-boy!

Ye blessed creatures, I have heard the call
      Ye to each other make; I see
The heavens laugh with you in your jubilee;
      My heart is at your festival,
        My head hath its coronal,

The fullness of your bliss, I feel—I feel it all.
        O evil day! if I were sullen
While Earth herself is adorning,
            This sweet May-morning,
        And the children are culling
            On every side,
        In a thousand valleys far and wide,
        Fresh flowers; while the sun shines warm,
And the babe leaps up on his mother's arm:—
        I hear, I hear, with joy I hear!
        —But there's a tree, of many, one,
A single field which I have look'd upon,
Both of them speak of something that is gone:
            The pansy at my feet
            Doth the same tale repeat:
Whither is fled the visionary gleam?
Where is it now, the glory and the dream?

                    WILLIAM WORDSWORTH. 1770–1850

Patriotism Innominatus

Breathes there the man with soul so dead,
        Who never to himself hath said,
    'This is my own, my native land!'
Whose heart hath ne'er within him burn'd
As home his footsteps he hath turn'd
        From wandering on a foreign strand?
If such there breathe, go, mark him well;
For him no Minstrel raptures swell;
High though his titles, proud his name,
Boundless his wealth as wish can claim;
Despite those titles, power, and pelf,
The wretch, concentred all in self,
Living, shall forfeit fair renown,
And, doubly dying, shall go down
To the vile dust from whence he sprung,
Unwept, unhonour'd, and unsung.

                SIR WALTER SCOTT. 1771–1832

Youth and Age

Verse, a breeze 'mid blossoms straying,
      Where Hope clung feeding, like a bee—
Both were mine! Life went a-maying
With Nature, Hope, and Poesy,
      When I was young!
When I was young?—Ah, woful When!
Ah! for the change 'twixt Now and Then!
This breathing house not built with hands,
This body that does me grievous wrong,
O'er aery cliffs and glittering sands,
How lightly then it flash'd along—
Like those trim skiffs, unknown of yore,
On winding lakes and rivers wide,
That ask no aid of sail or oar,
That fear no spite of wind or tide!
Naught cared this body for wind or weather
When Youth and I lived in't together.

Flowers are lovely! Love is flower-like;
Friendship in a sheltering tree;
O the joys, that came down shower-like,
Of Friendship, Love, and Liberty,
      Ere I was old!

Ere I was old? Ah, woful Ere,
Which tells me, Youth's no longer here!
O Youth! for years so many and sweet,
'Tis known that thou and I were one;
I'll think it but a fond conceit—
It cannot be that thou art gone!
Thy vesper-bell hath not yet toll'd—
And thou wert aye a masker bold!
What strange disguise hast now put on,
To make believe that thou art gone?
I see these locks in silvery slips,
This drooping gait, this alter'd size:

[157]

But springtime blossoms on thy lips,
And tears take sunshine from thine eyes!
Life is but thought: so think I will
That Youth and I are housemates still.

Dewdrops are the gems of morning,
But the tears of mournful eve!
Where no hope is, life's a warning
That only serves to make us grieve,
            When we are old!

That only serves to make us grieve
With oft and tedious taking-leave,
Like some poor nigh-related guest
That may not rudely be dismist.
Yet hath outstay'd his welcome while,
And tells the jest without the smile.

SAMUEL TAYLOR COLERIDGE. 1772–1834

Time, Real and Imaginary

On the wide level of a mountain's head
    (I knew not where, but 'twas some faery place),
Their pinions, ostrich-like, for sails outspread,
Two lovely children run an endless race,
      A sister and a brother!
      This far outstripp'd the other;
    Yet ever runs she with reverted face,
    And looks and listens for the boy behind:
      For he, alas! is blind!
O'er rough and smooth with even step he pass'd,
And knows not whether he be first or last.

SAMUEL TAYLOR COLERIDGE. 1772–1834

The Chestnut Casts His Flambeaux

The chestnut casts his flambeaux, and the flowers
    Stream from the hawthorn on the wind away,

The doors clap to, the pane is blind with showers.
　　Pass me the can, lad; there's an end of May.

There's one spoilt spring to scant our mortal lot,
　　One season ruined of our little store.
May will be fine next year as like as not:
　　Oh ay, but then we shall be twenty-four.

We for a certainty are not the first
　　Have sat in taverns while the tempest hurled
Their hopeful plans to emptiness, and cursed
　　Whatever brute and blackguard made the world.

It is in truth iniquity on high
　　To cheat our sentenced souls of aught they crave,
And mar the merriment as you and I
　　Fare on our long fool's-errand to the grave.

Iniquity it is; but pass the can.
　　My lad, no pair of kings our mothers bore;
Our only portion is the estate of man:
　　We want the moon, but we shall get no more.

If here to-day the cloud of thunder lours
　　To-morrow it will hie on far behests;
The flesh will grieve on other bones than ours
　　Soon, and the soul will mourn in other breasts.

The troubles of our proud and angry dust
　　Are from eternity, and shall not fail.
Bear them we can, and if we can we must.
　　Shoulder the sky, my lad, and drink your ale.

A. E. HOUSMAN. 1859–1936

Written in Northampton Asylum

I am: yet what I am none cares or knows,
　　My friends forsake me like a memory lost;
I am the self-consumer of my woes
　　They rise and vanish in oblivious host,

Like shades in love and death's oblivion lost;
And yet I am, and live with shadows tost

Into the nothingness of scorn and noise,
    Into the living sea of waking dreams,
Where there is neither sense of life nor joys,
    But the vast shipwreck of my life's esteems;
And e'en the dearest—that I loved the best—
Are strange—nay, rather stranger than the rest.

I long for scenes where man has never trod;
    A place where woman never smiled or wept;
There to abide with my Creator, God,
    And sleep as I in childhood sweetly slept:
Untroubling and untroubled where I lie;
The grass below—above the vaulted sky.

JOHN CLARE. 1793–1864

Swiftly Walk Over the Western Wave

Swiftly walk over the western wave,
    Spirit of Night!
Out of the misty eastern cave,
Where all the long and lone daylight
Thou wovest dreams of joy and fear,
Which make thee terrible and dear,—
    Swift be thy flight.

Wrap thy form in a mantle gray,
    Star inwrought!
  Blind with thine hair the eyes of Day;
Kiss her until she be wearied out,
Then wander o'er city, and sea, and land,
Touching all with thine opiate wand—
    Come, long sought!

When I arose and saw the dawn,
    I sighed for thee;

When light rode high, and the dew was gone,
And noon lay heavy on flower and tree,
And the weary Day turned to his rest,
Lingering like an unloved guest,
            I sighed for thee.

Thy brother Death came, and cried,
                Wouldst thou me?
Thy sweet child Sleep, the filmy-eyed,
Murmured like a noontide bee,
Shall I nestle near thy side?
Wouldst thou me?—and I replied,
                No, not thee!

Death will come when thou art dead,
            Soon, too soon—
Sleep will come when thou art fled;
Of neither would I ask the boon
I ask of thee, beloved Night—
Swift be thine approaching flight,
                Come soon, soon!

PERCY BYSSHE SHELLEY. 1792–1822

Man

Know then thyself, presume not God to scan,
The proper study of mankind is man.
Placed on this isthmus of a middle state,
A being darkly wise, and rudely great:
With too much knowledge for the sceptic side,
With too much weakness for the stoic's pride,
He hangs between; in doubt to act, or rest;
In doubt to deem himself a God, or beast;
In doubt his mind or body to prefer;
Born but to die, and reasoning but to err;
Alike in ignorance, his reason such,
Whether he thinks too little or too much:

L   [161]

Chaos of thought and passion, all confused;
Still by himself abused or disabused;
Created half to rise and half to fall;
Great lord of all things, yet a prey to all;
Sole judge of truth, in endless error hurled:
The glory, jest, and riddle of the world!

ALEXANDER POPE. 1688–1744

From Truth

Yon cottager, who weaves at her own door,
Pillow and bobbins all her little store,
Content, though mean; and cheerful, if not gay;
Shuffling her threads about the live-long day,
Just earns a scanty pittance; and at night
Lies down secure, her heart and pocket light:
She, for her humble sphere by nature fit,
Has little understanding, and no wit,
Receives no praise; but, though her lot be such,
(Toilsome and indigent) she renders much;
Just knows, and knows no more, her Bible true—
A truth the brilliant Frenchman never knew;

And in that charter reads, with sparkling eyes,
Her title to a treasure in the skies.
        O happy peasant! O unhappy bard!
His the mere tinsel, hers the rich reward;
He prais'd, perhaps, for ages yet to come;
She never heard of half a mile from home:
He, lost in errors, his vain heart prefers;
She, safe in the simplicity of hers.
        Not many wise, rich, noble, or profound
In science, win one inch of heav'nly ground.
And is it not a mortifying thought
The poor should gain it, and the rich should not?

WILLIAM COWPER. 1731–1800

Composed Upon Westminster Bridge
Sept. 3rd, 1802

Earth has not anything to show more fair:
Dull would he be of soul who could pass by
A sight so touching in its majesty:
This City now doth, like a garment, wear
The beauty of the morning; silent, bare,
Ships, towers, domes, theatres and temples lie
Open unto the fields, and to the sky;
All bright and glittering in the smokeless air.
Never did sun more beautifully steep
In his first splendour, valley, rock, or hill;
Ne'er saw I, never felt, a calm so deep!
The river glideth at his own sweet will:
Dear God! the very houses seem asleep;
And all that mighty heart is lying still!

WILLIAM WORDSWORTH. 1770–1850

O World Invisible, We View Thee

O world invisible, we view thee,
O world intangible, we touch thee,
O world unknowable, we know thee,
Inapprehensible, we clutch thee!

Does the fish soar to find the ocean,
The eagle plunge to find the air—
That we ask of the stars in motion
If they have rumour of thee there?

Not where the wheeling systems darken,
And our benumbed conceiving soars:—
The drift of pinions, would we hearken,
Beats at our own clay-shuttered doors.

[163]

The angels keep their ancient places;—
Turn but a stone, and start a wing!
'Tis ye, 'tis your estranged faces,
That miss the many-splendoured thing.

But (when so sad thou canst not sadder)
Cry;—and upon thy so sore loss
Shall shine the traffic of Jacob's ladder
Pitched between Heaven and Charing Cross.

Yea, in the night, my Soul, my daughter,
Cry,—clinging Heaven by the hems;
And lo, Christ walking on the water
Not of Gennesareth, but Thames!

FRANCIS THOMPSON. 1859–1907

The Burning Babe

As I in hoary winter's night
    Stood shivering in the snow,
Surprised I was with sudden heat,
    Which made my heart to glow;
And lifting up a fearful eye
    To view what fire was near,
A pretty Babe all burning bright
    Did in the air appear:
Who, scorched with exceeding heat,
    Such floods of tears did shed,
As though his floods should quench his flames,
    With what his tears were fed.
'Alas', quoth he, 'but newly born,
    In fiery heats I fry,
Yet none approach to warm their hearts
    Or feel my fire, but I.
My faultless breast the furnace is,
    The fuel wounding thorns,
Love is the fire, and sighs the smoke,
    The ashes shames and scorns;

The fuel justice layeth on,
    And mercy blows the coals,
The metal in this furnace wrought
    Are men's defiled souls;
For which, as now on fire I am
    To work them to their good,
So will I melt into a bath,
    To wash them in my blood.'
With this he vanished out of sight,
    And swiftly shrunk away,
And straight I called unto mind
    That it was Christmas Day.

ROBERT SOUTHWELL. 1560–1595

On His Blindness

When I consider how my light is spent
    Ere half my days, in this dark world and wide,
    And that one talent which is death to hide,
Lodged with me useless, though my soul more bent
To serve therewith my Maker, and present
    My true account, lest He returning chide;
    'Doth God exact day-labour, light denied?'
I fondly ask: but Patience, to prevent
That murmur, soon replies, 'God doth not need
    Either man's work or His own gifts; who best
    Bear His mild yoke, they serve Him best: His state
Is kingly; thousands at His bidding speed,
    And post o'er land and ocean without rest;
    They also serve who only stand and wait.'

JOHN MILTON. 1608–1674

Oft in the Stilly Night

Oft in the stilly night,
    Ere Slumber's chain has bound me,
Fond Memory brings the light

[165]

Of other days around me;
The smiles, the tears,
Of boyhood's years,
The words of love then spoken;
The eyes that shone,
Now dimmed and gone,
The cheerful hearts now broken!
Thus, in the stilly night,
Ere Slumber's chain has bound me,
Sad Memory brings the light
Of other days around me.

When I remember all
The friends, so linked together,
I've seen around me fall,
Like leaves in wintry weather;
I feel like one
Who treads alone
Some banquet-hall deserted,
Whose lights are fled,
Whose garlands dead,
And all but he departed!
Thus in the stilly night,
Ere Slumber's chain has bound me,
Sad Memory brings the light
Of other days around me.

THOMAS MOORE. 1779–1852

Last Lines

No coward soul is mine,
No trembler in the world's storm-troubled sphere
I see Heaven's glories shine,
And faith shines equal, arming me from fear.

O God within my breast,
Almighty, ever-present Deity!
Life, that in me has rest,
As I, undying Life, have power in Thee!

Vain are the thousand creeds
That move men's hearts: unutterably vain;
 Worthless as withered weeds,
Or idlest froth amid the boundless main,

 To waken doubt in one
Holding so fast by Thine infinity;
 So surely anchored on
The steadfast rock of immortality

 With wide-embracing love
Thy Spirit animates eternal years,
 Pervades and broods above,
Changes, sustains, dissolves, creates, and rears.

 Though earth and man were gone,
And suns and universes ceased to be,
 And Thou wert left alone,
Every existence would exist in Thee.

 There is not room for Death,
Nor atom that his might could render void:
 Thou—Thou art Being and Breath,
And what Thou art may never be destroyed.

                              EMILY BRONTE. 1819–1848

Invictus

Out of the night that covers me,
 Black as the pit from pole to pole,
I thank whatever gods may be
 For my unconquerable soul.

In the fell clutch of circumstance
 I have not winced nor cried aloud.
Under the bludgeonings of chance
 My head is bloody, but unbowed.

Beyond this place of wrath and tears
    Looms but the horror of the shade,
And yet the menace of the years
    Finds and shall find me unafraid.

It matters not how strait the gate,
    How charged with punishments the scroll,
I am the master of my fate;
    I am the Captain of my soul.

W. E. HENLEY. 1849–1903

Ode to the West Wind

I

O Wild West Wind, thou breath of Autumn's being,
Thou, from whose unseen presence the leaves dead
Are driven, like ghosts from an enchanter fleeing,

Yellow, and black, and pale, and hectic red,
Pestilence-stricken multitudes: O thou
Who chariotest to their dark wintry bed

The winged seeds, where they lie cold and low,
Each like a corpse within its grave, until
Thine azure sister of the Spring shall blow

Her clarion o'er the dreaming earth, and fill
(Driving sweet buds like flocks to feed in air)
With living hues and odours plain and hill:

Wild Spirit, which art moving everywhere;
Destroyer and preserver; hear, O, hear!

II

Thou on whose stream, 'mid the steep sky's commotion,
Loose clouds like earth's decaying leaves are shed,
Shook from the tangled boughs of Heaven and Ocean.

Angels of rain and lightning: there are spread
On the blue surface of thine airy surge,
Like the bright air uplifted from the head.

Of some fierce Mænad, even from the dim verge
Of the horizon to the zenith's height,
The locks of the approaching storm. Thou dirge

Of the dying year, to which this closing night
Will be the dome of a vast sepulchre,
Vaulted with all thy congregated might

Of vapours, from whose solid atmosphere
Black rain, and fire, and hail will burst: O, hear!

III

Thou who didst waken from his summer dreams
The blue Mediterranean, where he lay,
Lulled by the coil of his crystalline streams.

Beside a pumice isle in Baiæ's bay,
And saw in sleep old palaces and towers
Quivering within the wave's intenser day,

All overgrown with azure moss and flowers
So sweet, the sense faints picturing them! Thou
For whose path the Atlantic's level powers

Cleave themselves into chasms, while far below
The sea-blooms and the oozy woods which wear
The sapless foliage of the ocean, know

Thy voice, suddenly grow grey with fear,
And tremble and despoil themselves: O, hear!

IV

If I were a dead leaf thou mightest bear;
If I were a swift cloud to fly with thee;
A wave to pant beneath thy power, and share

The impulse of thy strength, only less free
Than thou, O uncontrollable! If even
I were as in my boyhood, and could be

The comrade of thy wanderings over heaven,
As then, when to outstrip thy skiey speed
Scarce seemed a vision; I would ne'er have striven

As thus with thee in prayer in my sore need.
O lift me as a wave, a leaf, a cloud!
I fall upon the thorns of life! I bleed!

A heavy weight of hours has chained and bowed
One too like thee: tameless, and swift, and proud.

V

Make me thy lyre, even as the forest is:
What if my leaves are falling like its own!
The tumult of thy mighty harmonies

Will take from both a deep, autumnal tone,
Sweet thou in sadness. Be thou, spirit fierce,
My spirit! Be thou me, impetuous one!

Drive my dead thoughts over the universe
Like withered leaves to quicken a new birth!
And, by the incantation of this verse,

Scatter, as from an unextinguished hearth
Ashes and sparks, my words among mankind!
Be through my lips to unawakened earth

The trumpet of a prophecy! O wind,
If Winter comes, can Spring be far behind?

PERCY BYSSHE SHELLEY. 1792–1822

[170]

From the Hymn of Empedocles

Is it so small a thing
To have enjoy'd the sun,
To have lived light in the spring,
To have loved, to have thought, to have done;
To have advanced true friends, and beat down baffling foes?

But thou, because thou hear'st
Men scoff at Heaven and Fate;
Because the gods thou fear'st
Fail to make blest thy state,
Tremblest, and wilt not dare to trust the joys there are.

I say, Fear not! life still
Leaves human effort scope.
But, since life teems with ill,
Nurse no extravagant hope.
Because thou must not dream, thou need'st not then despair.

MATTHEW ARNOLD. 1822–1888

Lines Written in Kensington Gardens

In this lone open glad I lie,
    Screen'd by dark trees on either hand;
And at its head, to stay the eye,
    Those black-topp'd, red-boled pine-trees stand.

The clouded sky is still and grey,
    Through silken rifts soft peers the sun,
Light the green-foliaged chestnuts play,
    The darker elms stand grave and dun.

The birds sing sweetly in these trees
    Across the girdling city's hum;
How green under the boughs it is!
    How thick the tremulous sheep-cries come!

[171]

Sometimes a child will cross the glade
　　To take his nurse his broken toy:
Sometimes a thrush flit overhead
　　Deep in her unknown day's employ.

Here at my feet what wonders pass,
　　What endless active life is here!
What blowing daisies, fragrant grass!
　　An air-stirr'd forest, fresh and clear.

Scarce fresher is the mountain sod
　　Where tired the angler lies, stretch'd out,
And, eased of basket and of rod,
　　Counts his day's spoil—the spotted trout.

I, on men's impious uproar hurl'd,
　　Think sometimes, as I hear them rave,
That peace has left the upper world,
　　And now keeps only in the grave.

Yet here is peace for ever new.
　　When I, who watch them, am away,
Still all things in this glade go through
　　The changes of their quiet day.

Then to their happy rest they pass.
　　The flowers close, the birds are fed;
The night comes down upon the grass;
　　The child sleeps warmly in his bed.

Calm Soul of all things! make it mine
　　To feel, amid the city's jar,
That there abides a peace of thine,
　　Man did not make, and cannot mar.

The will to neither strive nor cry,
　　The power to feel with others give.
Calm, calm me more; nor let me die
　　Before I have begun to live.

MATTHEW ARNOLD. 1822–1888

Song from 'Pippa Passes'

The year's at the spring,
And day's at the morn;
Morning's at seven;
The hill-side's dew-pearled;
The lark's on the wing;
The snail's on the thorn;
God's in His heaven—
All's right with the world.

ROBERT BROWNING. 1812–1889

Up at a Villa—Down in the City

I

Had I but plenty of money, money enough and to spare,
The house for me, no doubt, were a house in the city-square;
Ah, such a life, such a life, as one leads at the window there!

II

Something to see, by Bacchus, something to hear, at least!
There, the whole day long, one's life is a perfect feast;
While up at a villa one lives, I maintain it, no more than a beast.

III

Well now, look at our villa! stuck like the horn of a bull
Just on a mountain edge as bare as the creature's skull,
Save a mere shag of a bush with hardly a leaf to pull!
—I scratch my own, sometimes, to see if the hair's turned wool.

IV

But the city, oh the city—the square with the houses! Why?
They are stone-faced, white as a curd, there's something to take the
    eye!

[173]

Houses in four straight lines, not a single front awry;
You watch who crosses and gossips, who saunters, who hurries by;
Green blinds, as a matter of course, to draw when the sun gets
    high;
And the shops with fanciful signs which are painted properly.

V

What of a villa? Though winter be over in March by rights,
'Tis May perhaps ere the snow shall have withered well off the
    heights:
You've the brown ploughed land before, where the oxen steam
    and wheeze,
And the hills over-smoked behind by the faint grey olive-trees.

VI

Is it better in May, I ask you? You've summer all at once;
In a day he leaps complete with a few strong April suns.
'Mid the sharp short emerald wheat, scarce risen three fingers
    well,
The wild tulip, at end of its tube, blows out its great red bell
Like a thin clear bubble of blood, for the children to pick and sell.

VII

Is it ever hot in the square? There's a fountain to spout and splash!
In the shade it sings and springs; in the shine such foam-bows
    flash
On the horses with curling fish-tails, that prance and paddle and
    pash
Round the lady atop in her conch—fifty gazers do not abash,
Though all that she wears is some weeds round her waist in a sort
    of sash.

VIII

All the year long at the villa, nothing to see though you linger,
Except yon cypress that points like death's lean lifted forefinger.
Some think fire-flies pretty, when they mix i' the corn and mingle,
Or thrid the stinking hemp till the stalks of it seem a-tingle.

Late August or early September, the stunning cicala is shrill,
And the bees keep their tiresome whine round the resinous firs on
    the hill.
Enough of the Seasons,—I spare you the months of the fever and
    chill.

IX

Ere you open your eyes in the city, the blessed church-bells begin:
No sooner the bells leave off than the diligence rattles in:
You get the pick of the news, and it costs you never a pin.
By and by there's the travelling doctor gives pills, lets blood,
    draws teeth;
Or the Pulcinello-trumpet breaks up the market beneath.
At the post-office such a scene-picture—the new play, piping hot!
And a notice how, only this morning, three liberal thieves were
    shot.
Above it, behold the Archbishop's most fatherly of rebukes,
And beneath, with his crown and his lion, some little new law of
    the Duke's!
Or a sonnet with flowery marge to the Reverend Don So-and-so,
Who is Dante, Boccaccio, Petrarca, St Jerome, and Cicero,
'And moreover,' (the sonnet goes rhyming) 'the skirts of St Paul
    has reached,
Having preached us those six Lent-lectures more unctuous than
    ever he preached.'
Noon strikes,—here sweeps the procession! our Lady borne
    smiling and smart,
With a pink gauze gown all spangles, and seven swords stuck in
    her heart!
Bang-whang-whang goes the drum, tootle-te-tootle the fife;
No keeping one's haunches still: it's the greatest pleasure in life.

X

But bless you, it's dear—it's dear! fowls, wine, at double the rate.
They have clapped a new tax upon salt, and what oil pays passing
    the gate
It's a horror to think of. And so, the villa for me, not the city!
Beggars can scarcely be choosers: but still—ah, the pity, the pity!

Look, two and two go the priests, then the monks with cowls and
    sandals,
And the penitents dressed in white shirts, a-holding the yellow
    candles;
One, he carries a flag up straight, and another a cross with
    handles,
And the Duke's guard brings up the rear, for the better prevention
    of scandals:
Bang-whang-whang goes the drum, tootle-te-tootle the fife.
Oh, a day in the city-square, there is no such pleasure in life!

ROBERT BROWNING. 1812–1889

Hymn to the Night

I heard the trailing garments of the Night
    Sweep through her marble halls!
I saw her sable skirts all fringed with light
    From the celestial walls!

I felt her presence, by its spell of might,
    Stoop o'er me from above;
The calm, majestic presence of the Night,
    As of the one I love.

I heard the sounds of sorrow and delight,
    The manifold, soft chimes,
That fill the haunted chambers of the Night,
    Like some old poet's rhymes.

From the cool cisterns of the midnight air
    My spirit drank repose;
The fountain of perpetual peace flows there,—
    From those deep cisterns flows.

O holy Night! from thee I learn to bear
    What man has borne before!
Thou layest thy finger on the lips of Care,
    And they complain no more.

[176]

Peace! Peace! Orestes-like I breathe this prayer!
  Descend with broad-winged flight,
The welcome, the thrice-prayed-for, the most fair,
  The best-beloved Night!

HENRY W. LONGFELLOW. 1807–1882

Unsatisfied

'Only a housemaid!' She looked from the kitchen,—
  Neat was the kitchen, and tidy was she;
There at her window a semptress sat stitching;
  'Were I a semptress, how happy I'd be!'

'Only a Queen!' She looked over the waters,—
  Fair was her kingdom and mighty was she;
There sat an Empress, with Queens for her daughters;
  'Were I an Empress, how happy I'd be!'

Still the old frailty they all of them trip in!
  Eve in her daughters is ever the same;
Give her all Eden, she sighs for a pippin;
  Give her an Empire, she pines for a name!

OLIVER WENDELL HOLMES

A Psalm of Life

Tell me not in mournful numbers,
  'Life is but an empty dream!'
For the soul is dead that slumbers,
  And things are not what they seem.

Life is real! Life is earnest!
  And the grave is not its goal;
'Dust thou art, to dust returnest,'
  Was not spoken of the soul.

M   [177]

Not enjoyment, and not sorrow,
    Is our destined end or way;
But to act, that each to-morrow
    Find us farther than to-day.

Art is long, and Time is fleeting,
    And our hearts, though stout and brave,
Still, like muffled drums, are beating
    Funeral marches to the grave.

In the world's broad field of battle,
    In the bivouac of Life,
Be not like dumb, driven cattle!
    Be a hero in the strife!

Trust no Future, howe'er pleasant!
    Let the dead Past bury its dead!
Act,—act in the living Present!
    Heart within, and God o'erhead.

Lives of great men all remind us
    We can make our lives sublime,
And, departing, leave behind us
    Footprints on the sands of time;

Footprints, that perhaps another,
    Sailing o'er life's solemn main,
A forlorn and ship-wrecked brother,
    Seeing, shall take heart again.

Let us, then, be up and doing,
    With a heart for any fate;
Still achieving, still pursuing,
    Learn to labour and to wait.

HENRY W. LONGFELLOW. 1807–1882

The Fiddler of Dooney

When I play on my fiddle in Dooney,
    Folk dance like a wave of the sea;

My cousin is priest in Kilvarnet,
  My brother in Moharabuiee.

I passed my brother and cousin:
  They read in their books of prayer;
I read in my book of songs
  I bought at the Sligo fair.

When we come at the end of time
  To Peter sitting in state,
He will smile on the three old spirits,
  But call me first through the gate.

For the good are always the merry,
  Save by an evil chance,
And the merry love the fiddle,
  And the merry love to dance.

And when the folk there spy me,
  They will all come up to me
With 'Here is the fiddler of Dooney!'
  And dance like a wave of the sea.

WILLIAM BUTLER YEATS. 1865–1938

Time, You Old Gipsy Man

Time, you old gipsy man,
  Will you not stay,
Put up your caravan
  Just for one day?

All things, I'll give you,
Will you be my guest,
Bells for your jennet
Of silver the best,
Goldsmiths shall beat you
A great golden ring,
Peacocks shall bow to you,

Little boys sing,
Oh, and sweet girls will
Festoon you with may,
Time, you old gipsy,
Why hasten away?

Last week in Babylon,
Last night in Rome,
Morning, and in the crush
Under Paul's dome;
Under Paul's dial
You tighten your rein—
Only a moment,
And off once again;
Off to some city
Now blind in the womb,
Off to another
Ere that's in the tomb.

Time, you old gipsy man,
        Will you not stay,
Put up your caravan
        Just for one day?

                            RALPH HODGSON

In City Streets

Yonder in the heather there's a bed for sleeping,
        Drink for one athirst, ripe blackberries to eat;
Yonder in the sun the merry hares go leaping,
        And the pool is clear for travel-wearied feet.

Sorely throb my feet, a-tramping London highways,
        (Ah! the springy moss upon a northern moor!)
Through the endless streets, the gloomy squares and byways,
        Homeless in the City, poor among the poor!

London streets are gold—ah, give me leaves a-glinting
    'Midst grey dykes and hedges in the autumn sun!
London water's wine, poured out for all unstinting—
    God! For the little brooks that tumble as they run!

Oh, my heart is fain to hear the soft wind blowing,
    Soughing through the fir-tops up on northern fells!
Oh, my eye's an ache to see the brown burns flowing
    Through the peaty soil and tinkling heather-bells.

ADA SMITH

The Third Adam

Long long ago, GOD made the world and then HE fashioned
    man,
now here am I, the last of the race that dallied whilst time passed
    by.
Behold me, the Third Adam, the man whom all nature defies.
Behold me, last of the masters, Pride's hero, Pride's victim of
    crime.
  In procession in my mind I see, familiar faces fond and dear,
smiling they call and beckon to me, left alone 'midst ghosts of
    dread.
Deep in my heart wells a dark pool of tears, and Grief's icy
    breath chills my soul,
Who is left to weep for me? What mourner can weep at my
    grave,
as I mourn and grieve for my own loved ones? I'm alone and the
    world is dead.
  My father's son, I bear his name. My father's home was mine,
    world is dead.
his philosophy too, my inheritance, and his love for this fair
    land of ours.
In peace and war our country's fame and honour were known afar,
Tasting love and black hate, we knew joy, we knew pain,
we knew Death as a foe and a friend.
  But what purpose remains in these grim thoughts, am I not
in this world all alone? Nor can son of mine ponder these lonely
    words, No, there are none, not one after me.

The smoke of war has rolled away and the scene of ruin lies
clear.
I raise to GOD my burning eyes, I'm alone amid the dead.
Down the dark ways of the mind I stray, with yearning seeking sleep,
to sleep and dream, and dreaming find the peace such dreaming
brings.
A dreadful dew rains from the clouds, silent, fell, afflicting,
whilst the far-off sound of a lonely clock, that somehow escaped
the ruin.
tolls out in measured painful groans these last few drops of time.
Here was I born, Here too I dwelt and loved each stick and stone,
now all that remains is the faded dreams and the ache of love
dead evermore.
The land is quiet and the world is still, for the music of life has
gone
and I forget those bitter days when an insane world screamed
madly for war,
when those men mad with guilt, unleashed their engines of doom
and fires of hate swept over us all.
Now the tide has receded, I'm left high on the strand, alone
with my thoughts of the past,
and the end creeps upon me in radiation's sly death, sinews and
bone burn and die.
My feet are grown weary, each heartbeat is sore, each thought
too soon sinks in regret.
Oh how I long for the far-away days when we sang and we
laughed and we lived.
Even tears played their part for in sorrow our friends never failed
with their love to console.
But vain are these thoughts, vain are my sighs, GOD is LOVE
and I'm here at HIS WILL.
In joy soon I'll greet HIM, the end now is near, I am weakness,
and tiredness, and pain.
Just one moment longer |the Third Adam I'll be, all alone all
alone mid the dead. . . .
Ah! there, I can hear HIM, "Adam, Adam," HE calls
Oh sweet voice that has sweet words to say, There's the sound of
rejoicing,
millions are singing, that the sheep which was lost now is found!

A. E. O'GIOBALLAIN

ENGLAND

Forefathers

Here they went with smock and crook,
        Toiled in the sun, lolled in the shade,
Here they mudded out the brook
        And here their hatchet cleared the glade.
Harvest supper woke their wit,
Huntsman's moon their wooing lit.

From this church they led their brides,
        From this church themselves were led
Shoulder-high; on these waysides
        Sat to take their beer and bread.
Names are gone—what men they were
These their cottages declare.

Names are vanished, save the few
        In the old brown Bible scrawled;
These were men of pith and thew,
        Whom the city never called;
Scarce could read or hold a quill,
Built the barn, the forge, the mill.

On the green they watched their sons
        Playing till too dark to see,
As their fathers watched them once,
        As my father once watched me;
While the bat and beetle flew
On the warm air webbed with dew.

Unrecorded, unrenowned,
        Men from whom my ways begin,
Here I know you by your ground
        But I know you not within—
All is mist, and there survives
Not a moment of their lives.

[185]

Like the bee that now is blown
    Honey-heavy on my hand,
From the toppling tansy-throne
    In the green tempestuous land—
I'm in clover now, nor know
Who made honey long ago.

EDMUND BLUNDEN

England

. . . England, with all thy faults, I love thee still—
My country! and, while yet a nook is left,
Where English minds and manners may be found,
Shall be constrain'd to love thee. Though thy clime
Be fickle, and thy year most part deform'd
With dripping rains, or wither'd by a frost—
I would not yet exchange thy sullen skies,
And fields without a flower, for warmer France
With all her vines; nor for Ausonia's groves
Of golden fruitage, and her myrtle bowers.
To shake thy senate, and from heights sublime
Of patriot eloquence to flash down fire
Upon thy foes, was never meant my task:
But I can feel thy fortunes, and partake
Thy joys and sorrows, with as true a heart
As any thunderer there. And I can feel
Thy follies too; and with a just disdain
Frown at effeminates, whose very looks
Reflect dishonour on the land I love.
How, in the name of soldiership and sense,
Should England prosper, when such things, as smooth
And tender as a girl, all essenced o'er
With odours, and as profligate as sweet—
Who sell their laurel for a myrtle wreath,
And love when they should fight; when such as these
Presume to lay their hand upon the ark
Of her magnificent and awful cause?
Time was when it was praise and boast enough

In every clime, and travel where we might,
That we were born her children. Praise enough
To fill th' ambition of a private man,
That Chatham's language was his mother tongue,
And Wolfe's great name compatriot with his own,
Farewell those honours, and farewell with them
The hope of such hereafter! They have fall'n
Each in his field of glory; one in arms,
And one in council—Wolfe upon the lap
Of smiling Victory that moment won,
And Chatham, heart-sick of his country's shame!
They made us many soldiers. Chatham still
Consulting England's happiness at home,
Secured it by an unforgiving frown,
If any wrong'd her. Wolfe, where'er he fought,
Put so much of his heart into his act
That his example had a magnet's force,
And all were swift to follow whom all loved.
Those suns are set. Oh, rise some other such!
Or all that we have left is empty talk
Of old achievements, and despair of new . . .

WILLIAM COWPER. 1731–1800

Oxford

I see the coloured lilacs flame
    In many an ancient Oxford lane
    And bright laburnum holds its bloom
Suspended golden in the noon,
The placid lawns I often tread
Are stained and carpeted with red
Where the tall chestnuts cast their flowers
To mark the fleeting April hours,
And now the crowded hawthorn yields
Its haunting perfume to the fields
With men and maidens hurrying out
Along Port Meadow to The Trout,
There, by the coruscating stream

To drink and gaze, and gaze and dream;
An ageless dame leaves her abode
To caper down the Woodstock Road
And greet a Dean she used to know

A trifling sixty years ago.
Queer tricycles of unknown date
Are pedalled at a frightful rate
Their baskets bulge with borrowed books
Or terriers of uncertain looks.

Perpetual motion in The High
Beneath a blue and primrose sky
And cherry blossom like a cloud
Beside the traffic roaring loud,
While daffodils go dancing gold
In streets where time runs grey and old
And poets, sweating in the throng,
Can sometimes hear a blackbird's song:
All Oxford's spires are tipped with rose
A wind full magic sweetly blows
And suddenly it seems in truth
As if the centuries of youth
Are crowding all the streets and lanes
In April when the lilac flames.

T. LOVATT WILLIAMS

The Rolling English Road

Before the Roman came to Rye or out of Severn strode
The rolling English drunkard made the rolling English road,
A reeling road, a rolling road, that rambles round the shire,
And after him the parson ran, the sexton and the squire;
A merry road, a mazy road, and such as we did tread
The night we went to Birmingham by way of Beachy Head.

I knew no harm of Bonaparte and plenty of the Squire,
And for to fight the Frenchman I did not much desire;
But I did bash their baggonets because they came arrayed

To straighten out the crooked road an English drunkard made,
When you and I went down the lane with ale-mugs in our hands,
The night we went to Glastonbury by way of Goodwin Sands.

His sins they were forgiven him; or why do flowers run
Behind him; and the hedges all strengthening in the sun?
The wild thing went from left to right and knew not which was
    which,
But the wild rose was above him when they found him in the
    ditch.
God pardon us, nor harden us: we did not see so clear
The night we went to Bannockburn by way of Brighton Pier.

My friends, we will not go again or ape an ancient rage,
Or stretch the folly of our youth to be the shame of age,
But walk with clearer eyes and ears this path that wandereth,
And see undrugged in evening light the decent inn of death;
For there is good news yet to hear and fine things to be seen,
Before we go to Paradise by way of Kensal Green.

G. K. CHESTERTON. 1872–1936

Yorkshire's Five
Aire, Wharfe, Nidd, Ure and Swale

When I'se been by Tiber an' when I'se been by Seine,
Listenin' theer messages, I fain to hear agen
Secrets of home-watters, born amang moor-sedges,
Fallin' doon like sparklin' ale ower steean ridges.

An' when I'se been by Danube, an' when I'se been by Rhine,
Tryin' to onderstand 'em, my homin' heart 'ud pine
For t'music o' my ain becks 'at spring 'mang boggy peat,
Wheer lapwings cry an' moorlarks lift prayers sae pure an' sweet.

Missouri an' St. Lawrence, Volga an' Thames an' Dee,
All on 'em are varra fine, but niver t'same to me
As rivers 'at are singin' wheer my faither speech prevails,
A-crinklin' an' a-cranklin' doon my forsaken Dales.

DOROTHY UNA RATCLIFFE

[189]

Milton! Thou shouldst be living at this hour

Milton! thou shouldst be living at this hour:
        England hath need of thee: she is a fen
    Of stagnant waters: altar, sword, and pen,
Fireside, the heroic wealth of hall and bower,
Have forfeited their ancient English dower
        Of inward happiness. We are selfish men;
        O raise us up, return to us again,
And give us manners, virtue, freedom, power!
Thy soul was like a Star, and dwelt apart;
        Thou hadst a voice whose sound was like the sea:
        Pure as the naked heavens, majestic, free,
        So didst thou travel on life's common way,
In cheerful godliness; and yet thy heart
        The lowliest duties on herself did lay.

WILLIAM WORDSWORTH. 1770–1850

It is not to be thought of that the Flood

It is not to be thought of that the flood
        Of British freedom, which, to the open sea
        Of the world's praise, from dark antiquity
Hath flow'd, 'with pomp of waters, unwithstood,'—
Roused though it be full often to a mood
        Which spurns the check of salutary bands,—
        That this most famous stream in bogs and sands
Should perish; and to evil and to good
Be lost for ever. In our halls is hung
        Armoury of the invincible Knights of old:
We must be free or die, who speak the tongue
        That Shakespeare spake; the faith and morals hold
Which Milton held.—In everything we are sprung
        Of Earth's first blood, have titles manifold.

WILLIAM WORDSWORTH. 1770–1850

The South Country

When I am living in the Midlands,
    That are sodden and unkind,
I light my lamp in the evening:
    My work is left behind;
And the great hills of the South Country
    Come back into my mind.

The great hills of the South Country
    They stand along the sea,
And it's there, walking in the high woods,
    That I could wish to be,
And the men that were boys when I was a boy
    Walking along with me.

The men that live in North England
    I saw them for a day:
Their hearts are set upon the waste fells,
    Their skies are fast and grey;
From their castle-walls a man may see
    The mountains far away.

The men that live in West England
    They see the Severn strong,
A-rolling on rough water brown
    Light aspen leaves along.
They have the secret of the Rocks,
And the oldest kind of song.

But the men that live in the South Country
    Are the kindest and most wise,
They get their laughter from the loud surf,
    And the faith in their happy eyes
Comes surely from our Sister the Spring
    When over the sea she flies;
The violets suddenly bloom at her feet,
    She blesses us with surprise.

I never get between the pines
        But I smell the Sussex air;
Nor I never come on a belt of sand
        But my home is there.
And along the sky the line of the Downs
        So noble and so bare.

A lost thing I could never find,
        Nor a broken thing mend:
And I fear I shall be all alone
        When I get towards the end,
Who will there be to comfort me
        Or who will be my friend?

I will gather and carefully make my friends
        Of the men of the Sussex Weald,
They watch the stars from silent folds,
        They stiffly plough the field.
By them and the God of the South Country
        My poor soul shall be healed.

If I ever become a rich man,
        Or if ever I grow to be old,
I will build a house with deep thatch
        To shelter me from the cold,
And there shall the Sussex songs be sung
        And the story of Sussex told.

I will hold my house in the high wood,
        Within in a walk of the sea,
And the men that were boys when I was a boy
        Shall sit and drink with me.

                                        HILAIRE BELLOC

The Old Vicarage, Granchester

(Written in Berlin, 1912)

Just now the lilac is in bloom,
        All before my little room;
And in my flower-beds, I think,

Smile the carnation and the pink;
And down the borders, well I know,
The poppy and the pansy blow . . .
Oh! there the chestnuts, summer through,
Beside the river make for you
A tunnel of green gloom, and sleep
Deeply above; and green and deep
The stream mysterious glides beneath,
Green as a dream and deep as death.—
Oh, damn! I know it! and I know
How the May fields all golden show,
And when the day is young and sweet,
Gild gloriously the bare feet
That run to bathe . . .

     Du lieber Gott!

Here am I, sweating, sick, and hot,
And there the shadowed waters fresh
Lean up to embrace the naked flesh.
Temperamentvoll German Jews
Drink beer around; and there the dews
Are soft beneath a morn of gold.
Here tulips bloom as they are told;
Unkempt about those hedges blows
An English unofficial rose;
And there the unregulated sun
Slopes down to rest when day is done,
And wakes a vague unpunctual star,
A slippered Hesper; and there are
Meads towards Haslingfield and Coton
Where das Betreten's not verboten . . .
εἴθε Υενοίμην . . . would I were
In Grantchester, in Grantchester!—
Some, it may be, can get in touch
With Nature there, or Earth, or such.
And clever modern men have seen
A Faun a-peeping through the green,
And felt the Classics were not dead,
To glimpse a Naiad's reedy head,
Or hear the Goat-foot piping low . .

N   [193]

But these are things I do not know.
I only know that you may lie
Day long and watch the Cambridge sky,
And, flower-lulled in sleepy grass,
Hear the cool lapse of hours pass,
Until the centuries blend and blur
In Grantchester, in Grantchester . . .
Still in the dawnlit waters cool
His ghostly Lordship swims his pool,
And tries the strokes, essays the tricks,
Long learnt on Hellespont, or Styx;
Dan Chaucer hears his river still
Chatter beneath a phantom mill;
Tennyson notes, with studious eye,
How Cambridge waters hurry by . . .
And in that garden, black and white
Creep whispers through the grass all night;
And spectral dance, before the dawn,
A hundred Vicars down the lawn;
Curates, long dust, will come and go
On lissom, clerical, printless toe;
And oft between the boughs is seen
The sly shade of a Rural Dean . . .
Till, at a shiver in the skies,
Vanishing with Satanic cries,
The prim ecclesiastic rout
Leaves but a startled sleeper-out,
Grey heavens, the first bird's drowsy calls,
The falling house that never falls.

God! I will pack, and take a train,
And get me to England once again!
For England's the one land, I know,
Where men with Splendid Hearts may go;
And Cambridgeshire, of all England,
The shire for Men who Understand;
And of that district I prefer
The lovely hamlet Grantchester.
For Cambridge people rarely smile,
Being urban, squat, and packed with guile;

And Royston men in the far South
Are black and fierce and strange of mouth;
At Over they fling oaths at one,
And worse than oaths at Trumpington,
And Ditton girls are mean and dirty,
And there's none in Harston under thirty.
And folks in Shelford and those parts,
Have twisted lips and twisted hearts,
And Barton men make cockney rhymes,
And Coton's full of nameless crimes,
And things are done you'd not believe
At Madingley on Christmas Eve.
Strong men have run for miles and miles
When one from Cherry Hinton smiles;
Strong men have blanched and shot their wives
Rather than send them to St. Ives;
Strong men have cried like babes, bydam,
To hear what happened at Babraham.
But Grantchester! ah, Grantchester!
There's peace and holy quiet there,
Great clouds along pacific skies,
And men and women with straight eyes,
Lithe children lovelier than a dream,
A bosky wood, a slumbrous stream,
And little kindly winds that creep
Round twilight corners, half asleep.
In Grantchester their skins are white,
They bathe by day, they bathe by night;
The women there do all they ought;
The men observe the Rules of Thought.
They love the Good; they worship Truth;
They laugh uproariously in youth;
(And when they get to feeling old,
They up and shoot themselves, I'm told).

Ah God! to see the branches stir
Across the moon at Grantchester!
To smell the thrilling-sweet and rotten
Unforgettable, unforgotten
River smell, and hear the breeze

Sobbing in the little trees.
Say, do the elm-clumps greatly stand,
Still guardians of that holy land?
The chestnuts shade, in reverend dream,
The yet unacademic stream?
Is dawn a secret shy and cold
Anadyomene, silver-gold?
And sunset still a golden sea
From Haslingfield to Madingley?
And after, ere the night is born,
Do hares come out about the corn?
Oh, is the water sweet and cool
Gentle and brown, above the pool?
And laughs the immortal river still
Under the mill, under the mill?
Say, is there Beauty yet to find?
And Certainty? and Quiet kind?
Deep meadows yet, for to forget
The lies, and truth, and pain? . . . oh! yet
Stands the Church clock at ten to three?
And is there honey still for tea?

RUPERT BROOKE. 1887–1915

At Grafton

God laughed when He made Grafton
    That's under Bredon Hill,
A jewel in a jewelled plain.
The seasons work their will
On golden thatch and crumbling stone,
And every soft-lipped breeze
Makes music for the Grafton men
In comfortable trees.

God's beauty over Grafton
Stole into roof and wall,
And hallowed every paved path
And every lowly stall,

[196]

And to a woven wonder
Conspired with one accord
The labour of the servant,
The labour of the Lord.

And momently to Grafton
Comes in from vale and wold
The sound of sheep unshepherded,
The sound of sheep in fold,
And, blown along the bases
Of lands that set their wide
Frank brows to God, comes chanting
The breath of Bristol tide.

JOHN DRINKWATER

My Will

I would live, if I had my will,
In an old stone grange on a Yorkshire hill
Ivy-encircled, lichen-streaked,
Low and mullioned, gable-peaked,
With a velvet lawn, and a hedge of yew,
An apple orchard to saunter through,
Hyacinth-scented in spring's clear prime
And rich with roses in summer-time,
And a waft of heather over the hill,
Had I my will.

Over my tree-tops, grave and brown,
Slants the back of a breezy down;
Through my fields, by the covert edge,
A swift stream splashes from ledge to ledge
On to the hamlet, scattered, gray,
Where folk live leisurely day by day;
The same old faces about my walks;
Smiling welcomes and simple talks;
Innocent stories of Jack and Jill;
Had I my will.

[197]

How my thrushes should pipe ere noon,
Young birds learning the old birds' tune;
Casements wide, when the eve is fair,
To drink the scents of the moonlit air.
Over the valley I'd see the lights
Of the lone hill-farms, on the upland heights;
And hear, when the night is alert with rain,
The steady pulse of the labouring train,
With the measured gush of the merry rill,
                              Had I my will.

Then in the winter, when gusts pipe thin,
By a clear fire would I sit within,
Warm and dry in the ingle nook,
Reading at ease in a good, grave book;
Under the lamp, as I sideways bend,
I'd scan the face of my well-loved friend;
Writing my verses with careless speed,
One, at least, would be pleased to read;
Thus sweet leisure my days should fill,
                              Had I my will.

Then when the last guest steps to my side—
May it be summer, the windows wide—
I would smile as the parson prayed,
Smile to think I was once afraid;
Death should beckon me, take my hand,
Smile at the door of the silent land,
Then the slumber, how good to sleep
Under the grass where the shadows creep,
Where the headstones slant on the wind-swept hill!
                              I shall have my will!

ARTHUR C. BENSON

The Homes of England

The stately homes of England,
    How beautiful they stand
Amidst their tall ancestral trees,
    O'er all the pleasant land!

The deer across their greensward bound,
      Through shade and sunny gleam;
And the swan glides past them with the sound
      Of some rejoicing stream.

The merry homes of England!
      Around their hearths by night,
What gladsome looks of household love
      Meet in the ruddy light!
There woman's voice flows forth in song,
      Or childhood's tale is told,
Or lips move tunefully along
      Some glorious page of old.

The blessed homes of England!
      How softly on their bowers
Is laid the holy quietness
      That breathes from Sabbath hours!
Solemn, yet sweet, the church-bell's chime
      Floats through their woods at morn;
All other sounds, in that still time,
      Of breeze and leaf are born.

The cottage homes of England!
      By thousands on her plains,
They are smiling o'er the silvery brooks,
      And round the hamlet fanes.
Through glowing orchards forth they peep,
      Each from its nook of leaves;
And fearless there the lowly sleep,
      As the bird beneath their eaves.

The free fair homes of England!
      Long, long, in hut and hall,
May hearts of native proof be reared
      To guard each hallowed wall!
And green for ever be the groves,
      And bright the flowery sod,
Where first the child's glad spirit loves
      Its country and its God!

MRS. HEMANS. 1793–1835

Helpstone

Hail, humble Helpstone! where thy valleys spread,
And thy mean village lifts its lowly head,
Unknown to grandeur, and unknown to fame,
No minstrel boasting to advance thy name:
Unletter'd spot! unheard in poets' song,
Where bustling labour drives the hours along,
Where dawning genius never met the day,
Where useless ignorance slumbers life away,
Unknown nor heeded, where low genius tries
Above the vulgar and the vain to rise.

Hail, scenes obscure! so near and dear to me,
The church, the brook, the cottage, and the tree:
Still shall obscurity rehearse the song,
And hum your beauties as I stroll along.
Dear, native spot! which length of time endears,
The sweet retreat of twenty lingering years;
And, oh! those years of infancy the scene,
Those dear delights, where once they all have been,
Those golden days, long vanish'd from the plain,
Those sports, those pastimes, now belov'd in vain;
When happy youth in pleasure's circle ran,
Nor thought what pains awaited future man,
No other thought employing, or employ'd,
But how to add to happiness enjoy'd:
Each morning wak'd with hopes before unknown,
And eve, possessing, made each wish their own;
The day gone by left no pursuit undone,
Nor one vain wish, save that it went too soon;
Each sport, each pastime, ready at their call,
As soon as wanted they possess'd them all:
These joys, all known in happy infancy,
And all I ever knew, were spent in thee.
And who but loves to view where these were past?
And who, that views, but loves them to the last?
Feels his heart warm to view his native place,

A fondness still those past delights to trace?
The vanish'd green to mourn, the spot to see
Where flourish'd many a bush and many a tree?
Where once the brook, for now the brook is gone,
O'er pebbles dimpling sweet went whimpering on;
Oft on whose oaken plank I've wondering stood
(That led a pathway o'er its gentle flood),
To see the beetles their wild mazes run,
With jetty jackets glittering in the sun:
So apt and ready at their reels they seem,
So true the dance is figur'd on the stream,
Such justness, such correctness they impart,
They seem as ready as if taught by art.
In those past days, for then I lov'd the shade,
How oft I've sigh'd at alterations made,
To see the woodman's cruel axe employ'd,
A tree beheaded, or a bush destroy'd:
Nay e'en a post, old standard, or a stone
Moss'd o'er by age, and branded as her own,
Would in my mind a strong attachment gain,
A fond desire that there they might remain;
And all old favourites, fond taste approves,
Griev'd me at heart to witness their removes.

Sweet rest and peace! ye dear, departed charms,
Which industry once cherish'd in her arms;
When ease and plenty, known but now to few,
Were known to all, and labour had its due;
When mirth and toil, companions through the day,
Made labour light, and pass'd the hours away;
When nature made the fields so dear to me,
Thin scattering many a bush and many a tree;
Where the wood-minstrel sweetly join'd among,
And cheer'd my needy toilings with a song;
Ye perish'd spots, adieu! ye ruin'd scenes,
Ye well-known pastures, oft frequented greens!
Though now no more, fond Memory's pleasing pains,
Within her breast your every scene retains.
Scarce did a bush spread its romantic bower,
To shield the lazy shepherd from the shower;

Scarce did a tree befriend the chattering pie,
By lifting up its head so proud and high;
No, not a secret spot did then remain,
Throughout each spreading wood and winding plain,
But, in those days, my presence once possess'd,
The snail-horn searching, or the mossy nest.

Oh, happy Eden of those golden years
Which memory cherishes, and use endears,
Thou dear, beloved spot! may it be thine
To add a comfort to my life's decline,
When this vain world and I have nearly done,
And Time's drain'd glass has little left to run;
When all the hopes, that charm'd me once, are o'er,
To warm my soul in ecstasy no more,
By disappointments prov'd a foolish cheat,
Each ending bitter, and beginning sweet;
When weary age the grave, a rescue, seeks,
And prints its image on my wrinkled cheeks—
Those charms of youth, that I again may see,
May it be mine to meet my end in thee;
And, as reward for all my troubles past,
Find one hope true—to die at home at last!

JOHN CLARE. 1793–1864

'PARTY PIECES'

The London Nightingale

Sweet is the bird of evening
    Who in the dusky woods
Can with a voice extremely choice
    Produce in fact the goods;
On all the country songsters he
    May claim to put the lid;
I don't deny it; I should be
    An idiot if I did.

But, though he charms the poets
    To many a golden song
(They swallow him with joy and vim,
    Nor would I say they're wrong),
I sing the visitant of Town,
    Not of the bosky vale,
The bird who never lets you down,
    The Cockney nightingale.

Though wearied with his journey,
    His wild heart never pants
For some cool spot in Surrey, not
    To mention Kent or Hants;
He does not cotton to the spell
    Of spinney or of copse,
But seeks a pitch that's lit-up well
    And handy for the shops.

And then he starts his music
    As many a glowing pen
Informs the Press each year from S.
    W., say, or N.
He sings beside the roaring route
    Of lorry, tram and bus,
And for the searching taxi's hoot
    Declines to give a cuss.

[205]

Compare with him his brother
  Who gladdens dale and hill,
When in the vein, with jocund strain,
  Provided things are still,
But if the faintest sound is heard,
  A distant yapping pup,
A passing car, a rival bird,
  Will dry completely up.

Give me the bird of Finchley,
  Or Penge or Peckham Rye,
One who enjoys a first-class noise
  And beats it, good and high;
O among nightingales unique,
  Last night how well you sang
In all the pride of Cockney cheek
  Without the Cockney twang!

DUM-DUM

Doing the -Doo

I know a lively rooster whose enthusiastic song
Is wafted on the local breeze and goes it hot and strong,
But, though he crows as heartfully as ever rooster crew,
He gets across the -doodle, but is diddled by the -doo.

His voice, an operatic bass, is anything but weak;
His bearing has the promise of exceptional physique;
His critics (who are many) would declare they never knew
A happier equipment for accomplishing the -doo.

One might assume the mocking of his brothers in the roost
Would give his will to conquer this impediment a boost;
One might suppose his harem would be getting at him too
To bridge the gulf that separates the -doodle from the -doo.

But nothing seems to cause him the remotest shade of doubt;
He owns his limitations and the rest he goes without,
Apparently uplifted by the thought that there are few,
If any, who are like him in avoidance of the -doo.

[206]

I don't know how he got it; by a microbe in the blood
It may be, or perhaps his singing-master was a dud
Who didn't make him practise till he sang his phrases through
And learned to crown the -doodle with the culminating -doo.

But every blessed morning from the earliest ray of light
Till even he is muted by the soft approach of night,
Hour upon hour his maddening song is lifted to the blue
To drive an audience frantic by omission of the -doo.

O self-complacent rooster, I address you as a friend;
Your neighbours are a kindly lot, but patience has an end;
I hear them muttering darkly, and my best advice to you
Is! Take a breath at -doodle and go solid for the -doo.

DUM-DUM

Miss Thompson Goes Shopping

Miss Thompson at Home
        In her lone cottage on the downs,
        With winds and blizzards and great crowns
        Of shining cloud, with wheeling plover
        And short grass sweet with the small white clover,
        Miss Thompson lived, correct and meek,
        A lonely spinster, and every week
        On market-day she used to go
        Into the little town below,
        Tucked in the great downs' hollow bowl,
        Like pebbles gathered in a shoal.

She Goes a-Marketing
        So, having washed her plates and cup
        And banked the kitchen fire up,
        Miss Thompson slipped upstairs and dressed,
        Put on her black (her second best),
        The bonnet trimmed with rusty plush,
        Peeped in the glass with simpering blush,

[207]

From camphor-smelling cupboard took
Her thicker jacket off the hook
Because the day might turn to cold.
Then, ready, slipped downstairs and rolled
The hearthrug back; then searched about,
Found the basket, ventured out,
Snecked the door and paused to lock it
And plunged the key in some deep pocket.
Then as she tripped demurely down
The steep descent, the little town
Spread wider till its sprawling street
Enclosed her and her footfalls beat
On hard stone pavement; and she felt
Those throbbing ecstasies that melt
Through heart and mind as, happy, free,
Her small, prim personality
Merged into the seething strife
Of auction-marts and city life.

She Visits the Bootmaker
Serenely down the busy stream
Miss Thompson floated in a dream.
Now, hovering beelike, she would stop
Entranced before some tempting shop,
Getting in people's way and prying
At things she never thought of buying;
Now wafted on without an aim.
And thus in course of time she came
To Watson's bootshop. Long she pries
At boots and shoes of every size,
Brown football boots, with bar and stud,
For boys that scuffle in the mud,
And dancing-pumps with pointed toes
Glassy as jet, and dull black bows;
Slim ladies' shoes with two-inch heel,
And sprinkled beads of gold and steel.
'How anyone can wear such things!'
On either side the doorway springs
(As in a tropic jungle loom
Masses of strange thick-petalled bloom

[208]

And fruits misshapen) fold on fold
A growth of sandshoes rubber-soled,
Clambering the doorposts, branching, spawning
Their barbarous bunches like an awning
Over the windows and the doors.

Is Tempted

But, framed among the other stores,
Something has caught Miss Thompson's eye
(O wordliness, O vanity!),
A pair of slippers—scarlet plush.
Miss Thompson feels a conscious blush
Suffuse her face, as though her thought
Had ventured further than it ought.
But O that colour's rapturous singing
And the answer in her lone heart ringing!
She turns (O, Guardian Angels, stop her
From doing anything improper!).
She turns; and, see, she stoops and bungles
In through the sandshoes' hanging jungles,
Away from light and common sense,
Into the shop dim-lit and dense
With smells of polish and tanned hide.
Soon from a dark recess inside
Fat Mrs. Watson comes, slip slop,
To mind the business of the shop.
She walks flat-footed with a roll—
A serviceable, homely soul,
With kindly, ugly face like dough,
Hair as colourless as tow.
A huge Scotch pebble fills the space
Between her bosom and her face.
One sees her making beds all day.
Miss Thompson lets her say her say
—'So chilly for the time of year.
It's ages since we saw you here'—
Then, heart-a-flutter, speech precise,
Describes the shoes and asks the price.
'Them, miss? Ah, them is six-and-nine!'

o

Wrestles With Temptation
        Miss Thompson shudders down the spine
        (Dream of impossible romance).
        She eyes them with a wistful glance,
        Torn between good and evil. Yes,
        For half-a-minute, and no less,
        Miss Thompson strives with seven devils,
        Then soaring over earthly levels,
        Turns from the shoes with lingering touch—

And is Saved
        'Ah, six-and-nine is far too much!
        Sorry to trouble you. Good-day!'

She Visits the Fishmonger
        A little further down the way
        Stands Miles's fish shop, whence is shed
        So strong a smell of fishes dead
        That people of a subtler sense
        Hold their breath and hurry thence.
        Miss Thompson hovers there and gazes.
        Her housewife's knowing eye appraises
        Salt and fresh, severely cons
        Kippers bright as tarnished bronze;
        Great cods disposed upon the sill,
        Chilly and wet with gaping gill,
        Flat head, glazed eye, and mute, uncouth,
        Shapeless, wan, old-woman's mouth.
        Next, a row of soles and plaice,
        With querulous and twisted face,
        And red-eyed bloaters, golden-grey;
        Smoked haddocks ranked in neat array;
        A group of smelts that take the light
        Like slips of rainbow, pearly bright;
        Silver trout with rosy spots,
        And coral shrimps with keen black dots
        For eyes, and hard jointed sheath
        And crisp tails curving underneath.
        But there upon the sanded floor,
        More wonderful in all that store

Than anything on slab or shelf,
Stood Miles the fishmonger himself.
Foursquare he stood and filled the place.
His huge hands and his jolly face
Were red. He had a mouth to quaff
Pint after pint: a sounding laugh,
But wheezy at the end, and oft
His eyes bulged outwards and he coughed.
Aproned he stood from chin to toe.
The apron's vertical long flow
Warped grandly outwards to display
His hale, round belly hung midway,
Whose apex was securely bound
With apron-strings wrapped round and round.
Outside Miss Thompson, small and staid,
Felt, as she always felt, afraid
Of this huge man who laughed so loud
And drew the notice of the crowd.
Awhile she paused in timid thought,
Then promptly hurried in and bought
'Two kippers, please. Yes, lovely weather.'
'Two kippers? Sixpence altogether.'
And in her basket laid the pair
Wrapped face to face in newspaper.

Relapses into Temptation
Then on she went, as one half blind,
For things were stirring in her mind.
Then turned about with fixed intent,
And, heading for the bootshop, went

And Falls
Straight in and bought the scarlet slippers,
And popped them in beside the kippers.

She Visits the Chemist
So much for that. From there she tacked,
Still flushed by this decisive act,
Westward, and came without a stop
To Mr. Wren the chemist's shop,

[211]

And paused outside a while to see
The tall, big-bellied bottles, three—
Red, blue, and emerald, richly bright,
Each with its burning core of light.
The bell chimed as she pushed the door,
Spotless the oilcloth on the floor,
Limpid as water each glass case,
Each thing precisely in its place.
Rows of small drawers, black-lettered each
With curious words of foreign speech,
Ranked high above the other ware.
The old strange fragrance filled the air,
A fragrance like the garden pink,
But tinged with vague medicinal stink
Of camphor, soap, new sponges, blent
With chloroform and violet scent.
And Wren the chemist tall and spare
Stood gaunt behind his counter there.
Quiet and very wise he seemed,
With skull-like face, bald head that gleamed;
Through spectacles his eyes looked kind;
He wore a pencil tucked behind
His ear. And never he mistakes
The wildest signs the doctor makes
Prescribing drugs. Brown paper, string
He will not use for anything,
But all in neat white parcels packs
And sticks them up with sealing wax.
Miss Thompson bowed and blushed, and then
Undoubting bought from Mr. Wren,
Being free from modern scepticism,
A bottle for her rheumatism,
Also some peppermints to take
In case of wind; an oval cake
Of scented soap; a penny square
Of pungent naphthalene to scare
The moth. And after Wren had wrapped
And sealed the lot, Miss Thompson clapped
Them in beside the fish and shoes.
'Good-day,' she says, and off she goes.

Is Led Away by the Pleasure of the Town

Bee-like Miss Thompson, whither next?
Outside you pause awhile, perplext,
Your bearings lost. Then all comes back
And round she wheels, hot on the track
Of Giles the grocer; and from thence
To Emilie the milliner,
There to be tempted by the sight
Of hats and blouses fiercely bright.
(O guard Miss Thompson, Powers that Be,
From Crudeness and Vulgarity!)
Still on from shop to shop she goes
With sharp bird's-eye, inquiring nose,
Prying and peering, entering some,
Oblivious of the thought of home.

Is Convinced of Indiscretion

The town brimmed up with deep-blue haze,
But still she stayed to flit and gaze,
Her eyes a-blur with rapturous sights,
Her small soul full of small delights,
Empty her purse, her basket filled.
The traffic in the town was stilled.
The clock struck six. Men thronged the inns.
Dear, dear, she should be home long since.

And Returns Home

Then as she climbed the misty downs
The lamps were lighted in the town's
Small streets. She saw them star by star
Multiplying from afar;
Till, mapped beneath her, she could trace
Each street and the wide, square market-place
Sunk deep and deeper as she went
Higher up the steep ascent.
And all that soul-uplifting stir
Step by step fell back from her,
The glory gone, the blossoming
Shrivelled, and she, a small, frail thing,
Carrying her laden basket. Till

[213]

Darkness and silence of the hill
Received her in their restful care
And stars came dropping through the air.
But loudly, sweetly sang the slippers
In the basket with the kippers,
And loud and sweet the answering thrills
From her lone heart on the hills.

MARTIN ARMSTRONG

The Revenge

I

At Flores in the Azores Sir Richard
        Grenville lay,
And a pinnace, like a flutter'd bird, came
        flying from far away:
'Spanish ships of war at sea! we have
        sighted fifty-three!'
Then sware Lord Thomas Howard:
        'Fore God I am no coward;
But I cannot meet them here, for my
        ships are out of gear,
And the half my men are sick. I must
        fly, but follow quick.
We are six ships of the line; can we
        fight with fifty-three?'

II

Then spake Sir Richard Grenville: 'I
        know you are no coward;
You fly them for a moment to fight with
        them again.
But I've ninety men and more that are
        lying sick ashore.
I should count myself the coward if I left
        them, my Lord Howard,
To these Inquisition dogs and the devil-
        doms of Spain.'

[214]

So Lord Howard past away with five
       ships of war that day,
Till he melted like a cloud in the silent
       summer heaven;
But Sir Richard bore in hand all his sick
       men from the land
Very carefully and slow,
Men of Bideford in Devon,
And we laid them on the ballast down
       below;
For we brought them all aboard,
And they blest him in their pain, that they
       were not left to Spain,
To the thumbscrew and the stake, for the
       glory of the Lord.

IV

He had only a hundred seamen to work
       the ship and to fight,
And he sailed away from Flores till the
       Spaniard came in sight,
With his huge sea-castles heaving upon
       the weather bow.
'Shall we fight or shall we fly?
Good Sir Richard, tell us now,
For to fight is but to die!
There'll be little of us left by the time
       this sun be set.'
And Sir Richard said again: 'We be all
       good English men.
Let us bang these dogs of Seville, the
       children of the devil,
For I never turn'd my back upon Don or
       devil yet.'

V

Sir Richard spoke and he laugh'd, and
       we roar'd a hurrah, and so

The little Revenge ran on sheer into the
        heart of the foe,
With her hundred fighters on deck, and
        her ninety sick below;
For half of their fleet to the right and
        half to the left were seen,
And the little Revenge ran on thro' the
        long sea-lane between.

VI

Thousands of their soldiers look'd down
        from their decks and laugh'd,
Thousands of their seamen made mock at
        the mad little craft
Running on and on, till delay'd
By their mountain-like San Philip that,
        of fifteen hundred tons,
And up-shadowing high above us with
        her yawning tiers of guns,
Took the breath from our sails, and
        we stay'd.

VII

And while now the great San Philip hung
        above us like a cloud
Whence the thunderbolt will fall
Long and loud,
Four galleons drew away
From the Spanish fleet that day,
And two upon the larboard and two upon
        the star-board lay,
And the battle-thunder broke from them
        all.

VIII

But anon the great San Philip, she be-
        thought herself and went
Having that within her womb that had
        left her ill content;

And the rest they came aboard us, and
            they fought us hand to hand,
For a dozen times they came with their
            pikes and musqueteers,
And a dozen times we shook 'em off as a
            dog that shakes his ears
When he leaps from the water to the land.

IX

And the sun went down, and the stars
            came out far over the summer sea,
But never a moment ceased the fight of
            the one and the fifty-three.
Ship after ship, the whole night long,
            their high-built galleons came,
Ship after ship, the whole night long,
            with her battle-thunder and flame;
Ship after ship, the whole night long, drew
            back with her dead and her shame.
For some were sunk and many were shat-
            ter'd, and so could fight us no more—
God of battles, was ever a battle like this
            in the world before?

X

For he said 'Fight on! fight on!'
Tho' his vessel was all but a wreck;
And it chanced that, when half of the
            short summer night was gone,
With a grisly wound to be drest he had
            left the deck,
But a bullet struck him that was dressing
            it suddenly dead,
And himself he was wounded again in the
            side and the head,
And he said 'Fight on! fight on!'

[217]

XI

And the night went down, and the sun
       smiled out far over the summer sea,
And the Spanish fleet with broken sides
       lay round us all in a ring;
But they dared not touch us again, for
       they fear'd that we still could sting,
So they watch'd what the end would be.
And we had not fought them in vain,
But in perilous plight were we,
Seeing forty of our poor hundred were
       slain,
And half of the rest of us maim'd for life
In the crash of the cannonades and the
       desperate strife;
And the sick men down in the hold were
       most of them stark and cold,
And the pikes were all broken or bent,
       and the powder was all of it spent;
And the masts and the rigging were lying
       over the side;
But Sir Richard cried in his English pride,
'We have fought such a fight for a day
       and a night
As may never be fought again!
We have won great glory, my men!
And a day less or more
At sea or ashore,
We die—does it matter when?
Sink me the ship, Master Gunner—sink
       her, split her in twain!
Fall into the hands of God, not into the
       hands of Spain!'

XII

And the gunner said 'Ay, ay,' but the
       seamen made reply:
'We have children, we have wives,
And the Lord hath spared our lives.

We will make the Spaniard promise, if
          we yield, to let us go;
We shall live to fight again and to strike
          another blow.'
And the lion there lay dying, and they
          yielded to the foe.

XIII

And the stately Spanish men to their
          flagship bore him then,
Where they laid him by the mast, old
          Sir Richard caught at last,
And they praised him to his face with
          their courtly foreign grace;
But he rose upon their decks, and he cried:
'I have fought for Queen and Faith like
          a valiant man and true;
I have only done my duty as a man is
          bound to do:
With a joyful spirit I Sir Richard Gren-
          ville die!'
And he fell upon their decks, and he died.

XIV

And they stared at the dead that had
          been so valiant and true,
And had holden the power and glory of
          Spain so cheap
That he dared her with one little ship
          and his English few;
Was he devil or man? He was devil
          for aught they knew,
But they sank his body with honour down
          into the deep,
And they mann'd the Revenge with a
          swarthier alien crew,
And away she sail'd with her loss and
          long'd for her own;

When a wind from the lands they had
            ruin'd awoke from sleep,
And the water began to heave and the
            weather to moan,
And or ever that evening ended a great
            gale blew,
And a wave like the wave that is raised
            by an earthquake grew,
Till it smote on their hulls and their sails
            and their masts and their flags,
And the whole sea plunged and fell on
            the shot-shatter'd navy of Spain,
And the little Revenge herself went down
            by the island crags
To be lost evermore in the main.

ALFRED, LORD TENNYSON. 1809–1892

Avalon: Atomic Age

The lavatory, the lavatory,
That's where my secret self would flee
The only spot within the world
Where all my secret thoughts unfurled
Go voyaging on the solemn hush
That follows on the tug of flush.

A tiny chamber near the sky
Where Cistern sings the lullaby
And fancy ranges far and wide
Inviolate from those outside;
Where peace spreads like a sunlit tide
Submerging soul while there you bide
As safe and free and unoppressed
As in a Himalayan crest.

Others may speak of it with shame
May call it by some other name
'The Bathroom', 'Toilet', 'Gents' or 'Cloaks'

[220]

Or 'Like to wash your hands, dear folks . . .?'
But I regard it trebly blessed
For why? But you have surely guessed,
Because it is a holy place
Where one can seek the kind of grace
That heals the mind with matchless peace
Where noise is stilled and troubles cease
To tease, distract and agitate
The only place to contemplate,
An ideal place to whittle wit
And conjure with the Infinite.

Demolish lounge and dining-room
Consign the hall to nameless tomb
Lock up the bedrooms, burn the stairs
Chop up the bannisters in pairs
Yet spare the sanctuary—leaving me
My Avalon, my lavatory.

R. F. DELDERFIELD

Papa's Plea: Both Channels

I had a son and daughter once
And I was proud of each
For years I bore them shoulder-high
Found names for them—like 'Sugar-Pie'
But now they're out of reach.

They did not fall in love and flee
To Gretna, a la mode
They did not join a motor rally
Get themselves killed and swell the tally
Of victims of the road.

They did not grow and set up house
They did not emigrate
We did not wage domestic war
I did not show them both the door
For staying out too late.

And yet they're lost to me for good
Because of my decision
To fertilise their artless wit
And keep them both at home a bit
With two-way television.

By God I made an ill-judged move!
By God I made an error!
Imagine what its like to breed
Two human beings who thrive and feed
On networked quiz and terror?

They do not hear when I advise
Nor yet when I insist
And all the exercise they get
Is taking turns beside the set
To give the knob a twist.

It recks not what the channels yield
Suspense and laughter mingle
The six-gun bangs
The bandit hangs
And in between the Jingle.

Four solemn men debate a point
Then someone's job is guessed at
A Burnley plumber stands confused
To keep ten million souls amused
And find out what he's best at.

A film-star's life is probed and bared
For half the world to snigger
And down each dusty Western Street
The corpses clutter up the feet
The harvest of the trigger.

Full-bosomed wenches trill and squall
Full-bottomed wenches canter
And later on
An Oxford don
Investigates Atlanta.

The non-stop channel tides roll on
To stupefy the senses
The life that was—still is some say
Becomes with every passing day
The flimsiest of pretences

Oh, oblong-eye in burnished box
Dispenser of the brain-stroke
My licence money take at will
My books, my joy, my health—but still
Surrender me my ain folk.

R. F. DELDERFIELD

Speech of Henry V at the Siege of Harfleur

Once more unto the breach, dear friends, once more;
    Or close the wall up with our English dead!
In peace, there's nothing so becomes a man
As modest stillness and humility;
But when the blast of war blows in our ears,
Then imitate the action of the tiger—
Stiffen the sinews, summon up the blood,
Disguise fair Nature with hard-favoured rage:
Then lend the eye a terrible aspect;
Let it pry through the portage of the head,
Like the brass cannon; let the brow o'erwhelm it,
As fearfully as doth a galled rock
O'erhang and jutty his confounded base,
Swilled with the wild and wasteful ocean.
Now set the teeth, and stretch the nostril wide;
Hold hard the breath, and bend up every spirit
To his full height!—On! on, you noblest English,
Whose blood is fetched from fathers of war-proof!
Fathers, that like so many Alexanders,
Have, in these parts, from morn till even fought,
And sheathed their swords for lack of argument.
Dishonour not your mothers: now attest
That those whom you called fathers did beget you!

[223]

Be copy now to men of grosser blood,
And teach them how to war!—And you, good yeomen,
Whose limbs were made in England, show us here
The mettle of your pasture; let us swear
That you are worth your breeding: which I doubt not;
For there is none of you so mean and base,
That hath not noble lustre in your eyes.
I see you stand like greyhounds in the slips.
Straining upon the start. The game's afoot;
Follow your spirit: and, upon this charge,
Cry—'God for Harry! England! and St. George!'

WILLIAM SHAKESPEARE. 1564–1616

The Seven Ages

All the world's a stage,
And all the men and women merely players:
They have their exits, and their entrances;
And one man in his time plays many parts,
His acts being seven ages. At first, the infant,
Mewling and puking in the nurse's arms:
And then, the whining school-boy, with his satchel,
And shining morning face, creeping like snail
Unwillingly to school. And then, the lover
Sighing like furnace, with a woful ballad
Made to his Mistress' eyebrow. Then, a soldier,
Full of strange oaths, and bearded like the pard,
Jealous in honour, sudden and quick in quarrel,
Seeking the bubble reputation,
Even in the cannon's mouth. And then, the justice,
In fair round belly, with good capon lined,
With eyes severe, and beard of formal cut,
Full of wise saws and modern instances;
And so he plays his part. The sixth age shifts
Into the lean and slippered pantaloon;
With spectacles on nose, and pouch on side,
His youthful hose well saved, a world too wide
For his shrunk shank; and his big manly voice,

Turning again towards childish treble, pipes
And whistles in his sound. Last scene of all,
That ends this strange eventful history,
Is second childishness, and mere oblivion;
Sans teeth, sans eyes, sans taste, sans everything.

WILLIAM SHAKESPEARE. 1564–1616

Vitai Lampada

There's a breathless hush in the Close to-night—
    Ten to make and the match to win—
A bumping pitch and a blinding light,
    An hour to play and the last man in.
And it's not for the sake of a ribboned coat,
    Or the selfish hope of a season's fame,
But his Captain's hand on his shoulder smote:
    'Play up! Play up! and play the game!'

The sand of the desert is sodden red,—
    Red with the wreck of a square that broke;—
The Gatling's jammed and the Colonel dead,
    And the regiment blind with dust and smoke.
The river of death has brimmed his banks,
    And England's far, and Honour a name,
But the voice of a schoolboy rallies the ranks:
    'Play up! play up! and play the game!'

This is the word that year by year,
    While in her place the School is set,
Every one of her sons must hear,
    And none that hears it dare forget.
This they all with a joyful mind
    Bear through life like a torch in flame,
And falling fling to the host behind—
    'Play up! play up! and play the game!'

SIR HENRY NEWBOLT

Roundabouts and Swings

It was early last September nigh to Framlin'am on Sea,
An' 'twas Fair-day come to-morrow, an' the time was after tea,
An' I met a painted caravan adown a dusty lane,
A Pharaoh with his waggons comin' jolt an' creak an' strain;
A cheery cove an' sunburnt, bold o' eye and wrinkled up,
An' beside him on the splashboard sat a brindled Tarrier pup,
An' a lurcher wise as Solomon an' lean as fiddle-strings
Was joggin' in the dust along 'is roundabouts and swings.

'Goo'aday,' said 'e; 'Goo'-day,' said I; 'an' 'ow d'you find things
    go,
An' what's the chance o' millions when you runs a travellin'
    show?'
'I find,' said 'e, 'things very much as 'ow I've always found.
For mostly they goes up and down or else goes round and round.'
Said 'e, 'The job's the very spit o' what it always were,
It's bread and bacon mostly when the dog don't catch a 'are;
But lookin' at it broad, an' while it ain't no merchant king's,
What's lost upon the roundabouts we pulls up on the swings!'

'Goo' luck,' said 'e; 'Goo' luck,' said I; 'you've put it past a
    doubt;
An' keep that lurcher on the road, the gamekeepers is out';
'E thumped upon the footboard an' 'e lumbered on again
To meet a gold-dust sunset down the owl-light in the lane;
An' the moon she climbed the 'azels, while a nightjar seemed to
    spin
That Pharaoh's wisdom o'er again, 'is sooth of lose-and-win;
For 'up an' down an' round,' said 'e, 'goes all appointed things,
An' losses on the roundabouts means profits on the swings!'

PATRICK R. CHALMERS

Instigating Brutus to Oppose Cæsar

Honour is the subject of my story:
I cannot tell what you and other men
Think of this life, but for my single self,
I had as lief not be, as live to be
In awe of such a thing as I myself.
I was born free as Cæsar. So were you.
We both have fed as well, and we can both
Endure the winter's cold as well as he.
For once upon a raw and gusty day,
The troubled Tiber chafing with his shores,
Cæsar says to me, 'Dar'st thou, Cassius, now
Leap in with me into this angry flood,
And swim to yonder point?' Upon the word,
Accoutred as I was, I plunged in,
And bade him follow; so indeed he did.
The torrent roar'd, and we did buffet it
With lusty sinews, throwing it aside,
And stemming it with hearts of controversy.
But ere we could arrive the point propos'd,
Cæsar cry'd 'Help me, Cassius, or I sink.'
Then as Æneas, our great ancestor,
Did from the flames of Troy upon his shoulders
The old Anchises bear, so, from the waves of Tiber
Did I the tired Cæsar: and this man
Is now become a god, and Cassius is
A wretched creature, and must bend his body
If Cæsar carelessly but nod on him.
He had a fever when he was in Spain,
And when the fit was on him, I did mark
How he did shake: 'tis true, this god did shake;
His coward lips did from their colour fly,
And that same eye, whose bend doth awe the world,
Did lose its lustre; I did hear him groan:
Ay, and that tongue of his, that bade the Romans
Mark him, and write his speeches in their books,
Alas! it cry'd, 'Give me some drink, Titinius'—

As a sick girl. Ye gods! it doth amaze me,
A man of such a feeble temper should
So get the start of the majestic world,
And bear the palm alone!
     Why, man, he doth bestride the narrow world
Like a Colossus, and we potty men
Walk under his huge legs, and peep about,
To find ourselves dishonourable graves.
Men at some time are masters of their fates;
The fault, dear Brutus, is not in our stars,
But in ourselves, that we are underlings.
Brutus and Cæsar! What should be in that Cæsar?
Why should that name be sounded more than yours?
Write them together, yours is as fair a name;
Sound them, it doth become the mouth as well;
Weigh them, it is as heavy; conjure with them,
Brutus will start a spirit as soon as Cæsar.
Now, in the name of all the gods at once,
Upon what meats doth this our Cæsar feed,
That he is grown so great? Age, thou art sham'd;
Rome, thou hast lost the breed of noble bloods!
When went there by an age, since the Great Flood,
But it was fam'd with more than with one man?
When could they say, till now, who talk'd of Rome,
That her wide walls encompass'd but one man?
Oh! you and I have heard our fathers say,
There was a Brutus once, that would have brook'd
The infernal devil to keep his state in Rome,
As easily as a king!

WILLIAM SHAKESPEARE. 1564–1616

Othello's Address to the Senate

Most potent, grave, and reverend signiors,
My very noble and approved good masters,—
That I have ta'en away this old man's daughter,
It is most true; true, I have married her;
The very head and front of my offending
Hath this extent, no more. Rude am I in my speech,

[228]

And little blessed with the soft phrase of peace;
For since these arms of mine had seven years' pith,
Till now some nine moons wasted, they have used
Their dearest action in the tented field;
And little of this great world can I speak,
More than pertains to feats of broils and battle;
And therefore little shall I grace my cause,
In speaking for myself. Yet, by your gracious patience,
I will a round unvarnished tale deliver
Of my whole course of love; what drugs, what charms,
What conjuration, and what mighty magic
(For such proceeding I am charged withal),
I won his daughter with.
                              I do beseech you,
Send for the lady to the Sagittary,
And let her speak of me before her father:
If you do find me foul in her report,
The trust, the office, I do hold of you,
Not only take away, but let your sentence
Even fall upon my life.
        Ancient, conduct them: you best know the place.
And, till she come, as truly as to heaven
I do confess the vices of my blood,
So justly to your grave ears I'll present
How I did thrive in this fair lady's love,
And she in mine.
        Her father loved me; oft invited me;
Still questioned me the story of my life,
From year to year; the battles, sieges, fortunes,
That I have passed,
I ran it through, even from my boyish days,
To the very moment that he bade me tell it
Wherein I spoke of most disastrous chances;
Of moving accidents by flood and field;
Of hair-breadth scapes i' the imminent deadly breach;
Of being taken by the insolent foe
And sold to slavery; of my redemption thence,
And with it all my traveller's history
(Wherein of antres vast, and deserts idle,*

* Sterile, barren.

[229]

Rough quarries, rocks, and hills whose heads touch heaven
It was my hint to speak), such was my process;—
And of the Cannibals that each other eat,
The Anthropophagi, and men whose heads
Do grow beneath their shoulders. This to hear
Would Desdemona seriously incline;
But still the house affairs would draw her thence;
Which ever as she could with haste despatch,
She'd come again, and with a greedy ear
Devour up my discourse: which I observing,
Took once a pliant hour; and found good means
To draw from her a prayer of earnest heart,
That I would all my pilgrimage dilate,
Whereof by parcel she had something heard,
But not intentively: I did consent;
And often did beguile her of her tears,
When I did speak of some distressful stroke
That my youth suffered. My story being done,
She gave me for my pains a world of sighs:
She swore,—In faith, 'twas strange, 'twas passing strange;
'Twas pitiful, 'twas wondrous pitiful:
She wished she had not heard it; yet she wished
That heaven had made her such a man: she thanked me:
And bade me, if I had a friend that loved her,
I should but teach him how to tell my story,
And that would woo her. Upon this hint I spake:
She loved me for the dangers I had passed;
And I loved her that she did pity them.
This only is the witchcraft I have used;

WILLIAM SHAKESPEARE. 1564–1616

The Gift of Tritemius

Tritemius of Herbipolis, one day,
While kneeling at the altar's foot to pray,
Alone with God, as was his pious choice,
Heard from without a miserable voice,
A sound which seemed of all sad things to tell,
As of a lost soul crying out of hell.

[230]

Thereat the Abbot paused; the chain whereby
His thoughts went upward broken by that cry;
And, looking from the casement, saw below
A wretched woman, with grey hair a-flow,
And withered hands held up to him, who cried
For alms as one who might not be denied.

She cried, 'For the dear love of Him who gave
His life for ours, my child from bondage save—
My beautiful, brave first-born, chained with slaves
In the Moor's galley, where the sun-smit waves
Lap the white walls of Tunis!'—'What I can
I give,' Tritemius said: 'my prayers.'—'O man
Of God!' she cried, for grief had made her bold,
'Mock me not thus; I ask not prayers, but gold.
Words will not serve me, alms alone suffice;
Even while I speak perchance my first-born dies.'

'Woman!' Tritemius answered, 'from our door
None go unfed; hence are we always poor,
A single soldo is our only store.
Thou hast our prayers;—what can we give thee more?'

'Give me,' she said, 'the silver candlesticks
On either side of the great crucifix.
God well may spare them on His errands sped,
Or He can give you golden ones instead.'

Then spake Tritemius, 'Even as thy word,
Woman, so be it! (Our most gracious Lord,
Who loveth mercy more than sacrifice,
Pardon me if a human soul I prize
Above the gifts upon His altar piled!)
Take what thou askest, and redeem thy child.'

But his hand trembled as the holy alms
He placed within the beggar's eager palms;
And as she vanished down the linden shade
He bowed his head and for forgiveness prayed.
So the day passed, and when the twilight came

He woke to find the chapel all aflame,
And, dumb with grateful wonder, to behold
Upon the altar candlesticks of gold!

JOHN GREENLEAF WHITTIER. 1807–1892

A Musical Instrument

What was he doing, the great god Pan,
Down in the reeds by the river?
Spreading ruin and scattering ban,
Splashing and paddling with hoofs of a goat,
And breaking the golden lilies afloat
With the dragon-fly on the river.

He tore out a reed, the great god Pan,
From the deep cool bed of the river;
The limpid water turbidly ran,
And the broken lilies a-dying lay,
And the dragon-fly had fled away
Ere he brought it out of the river.

High on the shore sat the great god Pan,
While turbidly flowed the river;
And hacked and hewed as a great god can
With his hard bleak steel at the patient reed,
Till there was not a sign of a leaf indeed
To prove it fresh from the river.

He cut it short did the great god Pan,
(How tall it stood in the river!)
Then drew the pith, like the heart of a man,
Steadily from the outside ring,
And notched the poor dry empty thing
In holes, as he sat by the river.

'This is the way,' laughed the great god Pan
(Laughed while he sat by the river),
'The only way, since gods began
To make sweet music, they could succeed.'
Then dropping his mouth to a hole in the reed
He blew in power by the river.

Sweet, sweet, sweet, O Pan!
Piercing sweet by the river!
Blinding sweet, O great god Pan!
The sun on the hill forgot to die,
And the lilies revived, and the dragon-fly
Came back to dream on the river.

Yet half a beast is the great god Pan,
To laugh as he sits by the river,
Making a poet out of a man:
The true gods sigh for the cost and pain—
For the reed which grows never more again
As a reed with the reeds of the river.

ELIZABETH BARRETT BROWNING. 1809–1861

The Old Story

He was a guileless college youth,
That mirrored modesty and truth;
And sometimes at his musty room
His sister called, to chase the gloom.
One afternoon, while she was there,
Arranging things with kindly care,
As often she had done before,
There came a knock upon the door.
Our student, sensitive to fears
Of thoughtless comrades' laughing jeers,
Had only time to deposit
His sister in an old clothes closet,
Then haste the door to open wide:
His guest unbidden steps inside.
He was a cheery-faced old man,
And with apologies began
For calling, and then let him know
That more than fifty years ago,
When he was in his youthful bloom,
He'd occupied that very room;
So thought he'd take the chance, he said,

[233]

To see the changes time had made.
'The same old window, same old view—
Ha, ha! The same old pictures too!'
And then he tapped them with his cane,
And laughed his merry laugh again.
'The same old sofa, I declare!
Dear me! it must be worse for wear,
The same old shelves!' And then he came
And spied the cupboard door. 'The same—
Oh my!' A woman's dress peeped through.
Quick as he could, he closed it to.
He shook his head. 'Ah, ah! the same
Old game, young man, the same old game.'
'Would you my reputation slur?'
The youth gasped; 'That's my sister, sir.'
'Ah!' said the old man, with a sigh,
'The same old lie—the same old lie!'

ANONYMOUS

Ask and Have

'Oh, 'tis time I should talk to your mother,
Sweet Mary,' says I.
'Oh, don't talk to my mother,' says Mary,
Beginning to cry:
'For my mother says men are deceivers,
And never, I know, will consent;
She says girls in a hurry who marry,
At leisure repent.'

'Then, suppose I would talk to your father,
Sweet Mary,' says I.
'Oh, don't talk to my father,' says Mary,
Beginning to cry:
'For my father he loves me so dearly,
He'll never consent I should go—
If you talk to my father,' says Mary,
'He'll surely say, "No."'

[234]

'Then how shall I get you, my jewel?
Sweet Mary,' says I;
'If your father and mother's so cruel,
Most surely I'll die.'
'Oh, never say die, dear,' says Mary;
'A way now to save you I see:
Since my parents are both so contrary—
You'd better ask me!'

SAMUEL LOVER. 1797–1868

The Recruit

Sez Corporal Madden to Private M'Fadden:
　'Bedad, yer a bad 'un!
　Now turn out yer toes!
　Yer belt is unhookit,
　Yer cap is on crookit,
　Ye may not be dhrunk,
　But, be jabers, ye look it!
　　　Wan—two!
　　　Wan—two!
Ye monkey-faced divil, I'll jolly ye through!
　　　Wan—two!—
　　　Time! Mark!
Ye march like the aigle in Cintheral Parrk!'

Sez Corporal Madden to Private M'Fadden:
　'A saint it ud sadden
　To dhrill such a mug!
　Eyes front! ye baboon, ye!
　Chin up!—ye gossoon, ye!
　Ye've jaws like a goat—
　Halt! ye leather-lipped loon, ye!
　　　Wan—two!
　　　Wan—two!
Ye whiskered orang-outang, I'll fix you!
　　　Wan—two!—
　　　Time! Mark!
Ye've eyes like a bat!—can ye see in the dark?'

[235]

Sez Corporal Madden to Private M'Fadden:
  'Yer figger wants padd'n'—
  Sure, man, ye've no shape!
  Behind ye yer shoulders
  Stick out like two bowlders;
  Yer shins is as thin
  As a pair of pen-holders!
      Wan—two!
      Wan—two!
Yer belly belongs on yer back, ye Jew!
      Wan—two!—
      Time! Mark!
I'm dhry as a dog—I can't shpake but I bark!'

Sez Corporal Madden to Private M'Fadden:
  'Me heart it ud gladden
  To blacken yer eye.
  Ye're gettin' too bold, ye
  Compel me to scold ye,—
  'Tis halt! that I say,—
  Will ye heed what I told ye?
      Wan—two!
      Wan—two!
Be jabers, I'm dhryer than Brian Boru!
      Wan—two!—
      Time! Mark!
What's wur-ruk for chickens is sport for the lark!'

Sez Corporal Madden to Private M'Fadden:
  'I'll not stay a gadd'n
  Wid dagoes like you!
  I'll travel no farther,
  I'm dyin' for—wather;—
  Come on, if ye like,—
  Can ye loan me a quather?
      Ya-as, you,
      What,—two?

And ye'll pay the potheen? Ye're a daisy! Whuttoo!
     You'll do!
     Whist! Mark!
The Rigiment's flatthered to own ye, me spark!'

R. W. CHAMBERS. 1802–1871

Arabella and Sally Ann

Arabella was a school-girl,
    So was Sally Ann.
Hasty pudding can't be thicker
    Than two school-girls can.

These were thick as school-girls can be,
    Deathless love they swore,
Vowed that naught on earth should part them,—
    One forever more.

They grew up as school-girls will do,
    Went to parties, too,
And as oft before has happened,
    Suitors came to woo.

But as fate or luck would have it,
    One misguided man
Favoured blue-eyed Arabella
    More than Sally Ann.

And, of course, it made no difference
    That the laws are such
That he could not wed two women,
    Though they wished it much.

So a coolness rose between them,
    And the cause,—a man.
Cold was Arabella—very;
    Colder Sally Ann.

[237]

Now they call each other 'creature';
　　What is still more sad,—
Bella, though she won the treasure,
　　Wishes Sally had.

PAUL CARSON

Matilda

Who told lies, and was Burned to Death.

Matilda told such Dreadful Lies.
It made one Gasp and Stretch one's Eyes;
Her Aunt, who from her Earliest Youth,
Had kept a Strict Regard for Truth,
Attempted to Believe Matilda:
The effort very nearly killed her,
And would have done so, had not She
Discovered this Infirmity.
For once, towards the Close of Day,
Matilda, growing tired of play,
And finding she was left alone,
Went tiptoe to the Telephone
And summoned the Immediate Aid
Of London's Noble Fire-Brigade.
Within an hour the Gallant Band
Were pouring in on every hand,
From Putney, Hackney Downs, and Bow.
With Courage high and Hearts a-glow
They galloped roaring through the Town,
'Matilda's House is Burning Down!'
Inspired by British Cheers and Loud
Proceeding from the Frenzied Crowd,
They ran their ladders through a score
Of windows on the Ball Room Floor;
And took Peculiar Pains to Souse
The Pictures up and down the House,
Until Matilda's Aunt succeeded
In showing them they were not needed;
And even then she had to pay
To get the Men to go away!

It happened that a few Weeks later
Her Aunt was off to the Theatre
To see that Interesting Play
The Second Mrs. Tanqueray.
She had refused to take her Niece
To hear this Entertaining Piece:
A Deprivation Just and Wise
To Punish her for Telling Lies.
That Night a Fire did break out—
You should have heard Matilda Shout!
You should have heard her Scream and Bawl,
And throw the window up and call
To People passing in the Street—
(The rapidly increasing Heat
Encouraging her to obtain
Their confidence)—but all in vain!
For every time She shouted 'Fire!'
They only answered 'Little Liar!'
And therefore when her Aunt returned,
Matilda, and the House, were Burned.

HILAIRE BELLOC

Jim

Who ran away from his Nurse, and was eaten by a lion.

There was a Boy whose name was Jim;
His Friends were very good to him.
They gave him Tea, and Cakes, and Jam,
And slices of delicious Ham,
And Chocolate with pink inside,
And little Tricycles to ride,
And
       read him Stories through and through
And even took him to the Zoo—
But there it was the dreadful Fate
Befell him, which I now relate.

You know—at least you ought to know,
For I have often told you so—

[239]

That Children never are allowed
To leave their Nurses in a Crowd;
Now this was Jim's especial Foible,
He ran away when he was able,
And on this inauspicious day
He slipped his hand and ran away!
He hadn't gone a yard when—
                                    Bang!
With open Jaws a Lion sprang,
And hungrily began to eat
The Boy, beginning at his feet.
Now, just imagine how it feels
When first your toes and then your heels,
And then by gradual degrees,
Your shins and ankles, calves and knees,
Are slowly eaten, bit by bit.

No wonder Jim detested it!
No wonder that he shouted 'Hi!'
The Honest Keeper heard his cry,
Though very fat
                        he almost ran
To help the little gentleman.
'Ponto!' he ordered, as he came
(For Ponto was the Lion's name),
'Ponto!' he cried,
                        with angry Frown,
'Let go, Sir! Down, Sir! Put it down!'
The Lion made a sudden Stop,
He let the Dainty Morsel drop,
And slunk reluctant to his Cage,
Snarling with Disappointed Rage.
But when he bent him over Jim
The Honest Keeper's
                        Eyes were dim.
The Lion having reached his head,
The Miserable Boy was dead!

When Nurse informed his Parents, they
Were more Concerned than I can say:—

His Mother, as she dried her eyes,
Said, 'Well—it gives me no surprise,
He would not do as he was told!'
His Father, who was self-controlled,
Bade all the children round attend
To James' miserable end,
And always keep a-hold of Nurse
For fear of finding something worse.

HILAIRE BELLOC

Watching a Dinner

Oh! Johnnie! 'ere's a dinner party—Look at all them things!
Oh! look at all them dishes—Wot that powdered footman brings!
Well, if they eat all that there food—'Ow poorly they will be!
'Ere, jump upon my back, Johnnie!—Now, then, you can see!
Oh! Johnnie! look at that ole gent,—They've took 'is plate away!
Afore 'e's finished 'arf 'is food,—That is a game to play!
No! that ain't beer they're drinkin' of—Not likely, why, that's
    fizz!
Oh! look at that great pink thing there,—That's salmon fish, that
    is!
I think there's some mistake 'ere, Johnnie!—We ain't arst to-
    night!
We could a-pick'd a bit, eh! Johnnie?—We've got the appetite!
Seein' all that food there makes yer 'ungry, that it do!
We ain't 'ad no dinner-parties lately! Johnnie! me and you!
Oh! Johnnie! look at that ole gal,—With only 'arf a gown,
The hice she's swaller'd must 'ave cost,—Ah! well nigh 'arf-a-
    crown.
She's 'avin' 'arf a quartern now, and wants it, that she do,
When I've eat too much hice myself,—I've 'ad that feelin' too!
Oh! Johnnie! they've pulled down the blind,—I call it nasty
    mean.
They're all ashamed, that's wot they is,—Ashamed o' bein' seen.
A-eatin' all that food like that,—'Tain't decent, that it ain't!
We wouldn't pull no blinds down—if we'd 'arf o' their com-
    plaint!

Q

So come along, let's 'oof it, Johnnie,—'Oof it to the Strand,
Now don't yer go a-cryin', Johnnie,—'Ere, give me your 'and.
'Ungry, Johnnie? So am I,—We'll get a bob or two,
A-callin' 'Keb or kerridge, Captain!' Johnnie! me and you!

ANONYMOUS

The Highwayman

PART ONE

I

The wind was a torrent of darkness among the gusty trees,
The moon was a ghostly galleon tossed upon cloudy seas,
The road was a ribbon of moonlight over the purple moor,
And the highwayman came riding—
      Riding—riding—
The highwayman came riding, up to the old inn-door.

II

He'd a French cocked-hat on his forehead, a bunch of lace at his
    chin,
A coat of claret velvet, and breeches of brown doe-skin;
They fitted with never a wrinkle: his boots were up to the thigh!
And he rode with a jewelled twinkle,
      His pistol butts a-twinkle,
His rapier hilt a-twinkle, under the jewelled sky.

III

Over the cobbles he clattered and clashed in the dark inn-yard,
And he tapped with his whip on the shutters, but all was locked
    and barred;
He whistled a tune to the window, and who should be waiting
    there
But the landlord's black-eyed daughter,
      Bess, the landlord's daughter,
Plaiting a dark red love-knot into her long black hair.

IV

And dark in the dark old inn-yard a stable-wicket creaked
Where Tim the ostler listened; his face was white and peaked;
His eyes were hollows of madness, his hair like mouldy hay,
But he loved the landlord's daughter,
      The landlord's red-lipped daughter,
Dumb as a dog he listened, and he heard the robber say—

V

'One kiss, my bonny sweetheart, I'm after a prize to-night,
But I shall be back with the yellow gold before the morning light;
Yet, if they press me sharply, and harry me through the day,
Then look for me by moonlight,
      Watch for me by moonlight,
I'll come to thee by moonlight, though hell should bar the way.'

VI

He rose upright in the stirrups; he scarce could reach her hand,
But she loosened her hair i' the casement! His face burnt like a
    brand
As the black cascade of perfume came tumbling over his breast;
And he kissed its waves in the moonlight,
      (Oh, sweet black waves in the moonlight!)
Then he tugged at his rein in the moonlight, and galloped away
    to the West.

PART TWO

I

He did not come in the dawning; he did not come at noon;
And out o' the tawny sunset, before the rise o' the moon,
When the road was a gipsy's ribbon, looping the purple moor,
A red-coat troop came marching—
      Marching—marching—
King George's men came marching, up to the old inn-door.

II

They said no word to the landlord, they drank his ale instead,
But they gagged his daughter and bound her to the foot of her
    narrow bed;
Two of them knelt at her casement, with muskets at their side!
There was death at every window;
          And hell at one dark window;
For Bess could see, through her casement, the road that he would
    ride.

III

They had tied her up to attention, with many a sniggering jest;
They had bound a musket beside her, with the barrel beneath her
    breast!
'Now keep good watch!' and they kissed her.
          She heard the dead man say—
Look for me by moonlight;
          Watch for me by moonlight;
I'll come to thee by moonlight, though hell should bar the way!

IV

She twisted her hands behind her; but all the knots held good!
She writhed her hands till her fingers were wet with sweat or
    blood!
They stretched and strained in the darkness, and the hours crawled
    by like years,
Till, now, on the stroke of midnight,
          Cold, on the stroke of midnight,
The tip of one finger touched it! The trigger at least was hers!

V

The tip of one finger touched it; she strove no more for the rest!
Up, she stood up to attention, with the barrel beneath her breast,
She would not risk their hearing; she would not strive again;
For the road lay bare in the moonlight;
          Blank and bare in the moonlight;
And the blood of her veins in the moonlight throbbed to her
    love's refrain.

VI

Tlot-tlot; tlot-tlot! Had they heard it? The horse-hoofs ringing
    clear;
Tlot-tlot, tlot-tlot, in the distance? Were they deaf that they did
    not hear?
Down the ribbon of moonlight, over the brow of the hill,
The highwayman came riding,
          Riding, riding!
The red-coats looked to their priming! She stood up, straight and
    still!

VII

Tlot-tlot, in the frosty silence! Tlot-tlot, in the echoing night!
Nearer he came and nearer! Her face was like a light!
Her eyes grew wide for a moment; she drew one last deep breath,
Then her finger moved in the moonlight,
          Her musket shattered the moonlight,
Shattered her breast in the moonlight and warned him—with her
    death.

VIII

He turned; he spurred to the Westward; he did not know who
    stood
Bowed, with her head o'er the musket, drenched with her own
    red blood!
Not till the dawn he heard it, and slowly blanched to hear
How Bess, the landlord's daughter,
          The landlord's black-eyed daughter,
Had watched for her love in the moonlight, and died in the
    darkness there.

IX

Back, he spurred like a madman, shrieking a curse to the sky,
With the white road smoking behind him, and his rapier bran-
    dished high!
Blood-red were his spurs i' the golden noon; wine-red was his
    velvet coat;

When they shot him down on the highway,
    Down like a dog on the highway,
And he lay in his blood on the highway, with the bunch of lace
    at his throat.

X

And still of a winter's night, they say, when the wind is in the
    trees,
When the moon is a ghostly galleon tossed upon cloudy seas,
When the road is a ribbon of moonlight over the purple moor,
A highwayman comes riding—
        Riding—riding—
A highwayman comes riding, up to the old inn-door.

XI

Over the cobbles he clatters and clangs in the dark inn-yard;
And he taps with his whip on the shutters, but all is locked and
    barred;
He whistles a tune to the window, and who should be waiting
    there,
But the landlord's black-eyed daughter,
        Bess, the landlord's daughter,
Plaiting a dark red love-knot into her long black hair.

ALFRED NOYES

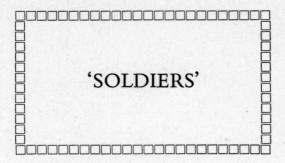

'SOLDIERS'

The Turkish Trench Dog

Night held me as I crawled and scrambled near
    The Turkish lines. Above, the mocking stars
Silvered the curving parapet, and clear
Cloud-latticed beams o'erflecked the land with bars;
I, crouching, lay between
Tense-listening armies, peering through the night,
Twin giants bound by tentacles unseen.
Here in dim-shadowed light
I saw him, as a sudden movement turned
His eyes towards me, glowing eyes that burned
A moment ere his snuffling muzzle found
My trail; and then as serpents mesmerise
He chained me with those unrelenting eyes,
That muscle-sliding rhythm, knit and bound
In spared-limbed symmetry, those perfect jaws
And soft-approaching pitter-patter paws.
Nearer and nearer like a wolf he crept—
That moment had my swift revolver leapt—
But terror seized me, terror born of shame
Brought flooding revelation. For he came
As one who offers comradeship deserved,
An open ally of the human race,
And sniffing at my prostrate form unnerved
He licked my face!

GEOFFREY DEARMER

A Twentieth Century Valediction

I've got new weapons, mother, in my pack,
As good as money can buy
To improve my chances of getting there and back.
Mother, don't cry.

Everything's improved, mother, since last time:
Methods can be relied upon:

Much better fire-power, range and rate-of-climb.
Mother, don't take on.

God rest your soul, mother and mine. With arms
Good training and plenty of spares,
We'll win hands down—but thanks for the lucky charms.
Mother, say your prayers.

JOHN PUDNEY

Dreamers

Soldiers are citizens of death's grey land,
    Drawing no dividend from time's to-morrows.
In the great hour of destiny they stand,
    Each with his feuds, and jealousies, and sorrows.
Soldiers are sworn to action; they must win
    Some flaming, fatal climax with their lives.
Soldiers are dreamers; when the guns begin
    They think of firelit homes, clean beds, and wives.
I see them in foul dug-outs, gnawed by rats,
    And in the ruined trenches, lashed with rain,
Dreaming of things they did with balls and bats,
    And mocked by hopeless longing to regain
Bank-holidays, and picture shows, and spats,
    And going to the office in the train.

SIEGFRIED SASSOON

Lost in France

He had the plowman's strength
In the grasp of his hand.
He could see a crow
Three miles away,
And the trout beneath the stone.
He could hear the green oats growing,
And the sou'-west making rain;
And the wheel upon the hill

[250]

When it left the level road.
He could make a gate, and dig a pit,
And plow as straight as stone can fall.
And he is dead.

Chant-Pagan

Me that 'ave been what I've been,
Me that 'ave gone where I've gone,
Me that 'ave seen what I've seen—
   'Ow can I ever take on
With awful old England again,
An' 'ouses both sides of the street,
And 'edges two sides of the lane,
And the parson an' 'gentry' between,
An' touchin' my 'at when we meet—
   Me that 'ave been what I've been?

Me that 'ave watched 'arf a world
'Eave up all shiny with dew,
Kopje on kop to the sun,
An' as soon as the mist let 'em through
Our 'elios winkin' like fun—
Three sides of a ninety-mile square,
Over valleys as big as a shire—
Are ye there? Are ye there? Are ye there?
An' then the blind drum of our fire . . .
An' I'm rollin' 'is lawns for the Squire,
                 Me!

Me that 'ave rode through the dark
Forty mile often on end,
Along the Ma'ollisberg Range,
With only the stars for my mark
An' only the night for my friend,
An' things runnin' off as you pass,
An' things jumpin' up in the grass,

An' the silence, the shine an' the size
Of the 'igh, inexpressible skies. . . .
I am takin' some letters almost
As much as a mile, to the post,
An' 'mind you come back with the change!'
                                    Me!

Me that saw Barberton took,
When we dropped through the clouds on their 'ead,
An' they 'ove the guns over and fled—
Me that was through Di'mond 'Ill,
An' Pieters an' Springs an' Belfast—
From Dundee to Vereeniging all!
Me that stuck out to the last
(An' five bloomin' bars on my chest)—
I am doin' my Sunday-school best,
By the 'elp of the Squire an' 'is wife
(Not to mention the 'ousemaid an' cook),
To come in an' 'ands up an' be still,
An' honestly work for my bread,
My livin' in that state of life
To which it shall please God to call
                                    Me!

Me that 'ave followed my trade
In the place where the lightnin's are made,
'Twixt the Rains and the Sun and the Moon;
Me that lay daown an' got up
Three years an' the sky for my roof—
That 'ave ridden my 'unger an' thirst
Six thousand raw mile on the hoof,
With the Vaal and the Orange for cup,
An' the Brandwater Basin for dish,—
Oh! it's 'ard to be'ave as they wish,
(Too 'ard, an' a little too soon),
I'll 'ave to think over it first—
                                    Me!

I will arise an' get 'ence;—
I will trek South and make sure

If it's only my fancy or not
That the sunshine of England is pale,
And the breezes of England are stale,
An' there's somethin' gone small with the lot;
For I know of a sun an' a wind,
An' some plains and a mountain be'ind,
An' some graves by a barb-wire fence;
An' a Dutchman I've fought 'oo might give
Me a job were I ever inclined,
To look in an offsaddle an' live
Where there's neither a road nor a tree—
But only my Maker an' me,
And I think it will kill me or cure,
So I think I will go there an' see.

RUDYARD KIPLING

Agincourt

Fair stood the wind for France
        When we our sails advance,
Nor now to prove our chance
        Longer will tarry;
But putting to the main,
At Caux, the mouth of Seine,
With all his martial train
        Landed King Harry.

And taking many a fort,
Furnish'd in warlike sort,
Marcheth tow'rds Agincourt
        In happy hour;
Skirmishing day by day
With those that stopp'd his way,
Where the French gen'ral lay
        With all his power.

Which in his height of pride,
King Henry to deride,
His ransom to provide

Unto him sending;
Which he neglects the while
As from a nation vile,
Yet with an angry smile
Their fall portending.

And turning to his men,
Quoth our brave Henry then,
'Though they to one be ten
Be not amazed:
Yet have we well begun;
Battles so bravely won
Have ever to the sun
By fame been raised.

'And for myself (quoth he)
This my full rest shall be:
England ne'er mourn for me
Nor more esteem me:
Victor I will remain
Or on this earth lie slain,
Never shall she sustain
Loss to redeem me.

'Poitiers and Cressy tell,
When most their pride did swell,
Under our swords they fell:
No less our skill is
Than when our grandsire-great,
Claiming the regal seat,
By many a warlike feat
Lopp'd the French lilies.

The Duke of York so dread
The eager vaward led;
With the main Henry sped
Among his henchmen.
Exeter had the rear,
A braver man not there;
O Lord, how hot they were
On the false Frenchmen!

They now to fight are gone,
Armour on armour shone,
Drum now to drum did groan,
    To hear was wonder;
That with the cries they make
The very earth did shake:
Trumpet to trumpet spake,
Thunder to thunder.

Well it thine age became,
O noble Erpingham,
Which didst the signal aim
    To our hid forces!
When from a meadow by,
Like a storm suddenly
The English archery
    Stuck the French horses.

With Spanish yew so strong,
Arrows a cloth-yard long
That like to serpents stung,
    Piercing the weather;
None from his fellow starts,
But playing manly parts,
And like true English hearts
    Stuck close together.

When down their bows they threw,
And forth their bilbos drew,
And on the French they flew,
    Not one was tardy;
Arms were from shoulders sent,
Scalps to the teeth were rent,
Down the French peasants went—
    Our men were hardy.

This while our noble king,
His broadsword brandishing,
Down the French host did ding
    As to o'erwhelm it;

[255]

And many a deep wound lent,
His arms with blood besprent,
And many a cruel dent
    Bruised his helmet.

Gloster, that duke so good,
Next of the royal blood,
For famous England stood
    With his brave brother;
Clarence, in steel so bright,
Though but a maiden knight,
Yet in that furious fight
    Scarce such another.

Warwick in blood did wade,
Oxford the foe invade,
And cruel slaughter made
    Still as they ran up;
Suffolk his axe did ply,
Beaumont and Willoughby
Bare them right doughtily,
    Ferrers and Fanhope.

Upon Saint Crispin's Day
Fought was this noble fray,
Which fame did not delay
    To England to carry.
O when shall English men
With such acts fill a pen?
Or England breed again
    Such a King Harry?

MICHAEL DRAYTON. 1563–1631

Before Action

By all the glories of the day
    And the cool evening's benison,
By that last sunset touch that lay
    Upon the hills when day was done,

By beauty lavishly outpoured
    And blessings carelessly received,
    By all the days that I have lived,
Make me a soldier, Lord.

   By all of all man's hopes and fears,
    And all the wonders poets sing,
The laughter of unclouded years,
    And every sad and lovely thing;
By the romantic ages stored
    With high endeavour that was his,
    By all his mad catastrophes,
Make me a man, O Lord.

I, that on my familiar hill
    Saw with uncomprehending eyes
A hundred of thy sunsets spill
    Their fresh and sanguine sacrifice,
Ere the sun swings his noonday sword
    Must say good-bye to all of this;—
    By all delights that I shall miss,
Help me to die, O Lord.

WILLIAM NOEL HODGSON

Into Battle

The naked earth is warm with spring,
    And with green grass and bursting trees
Leans to the sun's gaze glorying,
    And quivers in the sunny breeze;
And life is colour and warmth and light,
    And a striving evermore for these;
And he is dead who will not fight;
    And who dies fighting has increase.

The fighting man shall from the sun
    Take warmth, and life from the glowing earth;
Speed with the light-foot winds to run,

And with the trees to newer birth;
And find, when fighting shall be done,
    Great rest, and fullness after dearth.

All the bright company of Heaven
    Hold him in their high comradeship,
The Dog-Star, and the Sisters Seven,
    Orion's Belt and sworded hip.

The woodland trees that stand together,
    They stand to him each one a friend;
They gently speak in the windy weather;
    They guide to valley and ridge's end.

The kestrel hovering by day,
    And the little owls that call by night,
Bid him be swift and keen as they,
    As keen of ear, as swift of sight.

The blackbird sings to him, 'Brother, brother,
    If this be the last song you shall sing,
Sing well, for you may not sing another;
    Brother, sing.'

In dreary, doubtful, waiting hours,
    Before the brazen frenzy starts,
The horses show him nobler powers;
    O patient eyes, courageous hearts!

And when the burning moment breaks,
    And all things else are out of mind,
And only joy of battle takes
    Him by the throat, and makes him blind.

Through joy and blindness he shall know,
    Not caring much to know, that still
Nor lead nor steel shall reach him, so
    That it be not the Destined Will.

The thundering line of battle stands,
    And in the air death moans and sings;
But Day shall clasp him with strong hands,
    And Night shall fold him in soft wings.

JULIAN GRENFELL. 1888–1915

Home Thoughts in Laventie

    Green gardens in Laventie!
      Soldiers only know the street
Where the mud is churned and splashed about
      By battle-wending feet;
And yet beside one stricken house there is a glimpse of grass.
      Look for it when you pass.

    Beyond the church whose pitted spire
      Seems balanced on a strand
Of swaying stone and tottering brick
      Two roofless ruins stand,
And here behind the wreckage where the back wall should have
    been
      We found a garden green.

    The grass was never trodden on,
      The little path of gravel
Was overgrown with celandine,
      No other folk did travel
Along its weedy surface, but the nimble-footed mouse
      Running from house to house.

    So all among the vivid blades
      Of soft and tender grass
We lay, nor heard the limber wheels
      That pass and ever pass
In noisy continuity until their very rattle
      Seems in itself a battle.

    At length we rose up from this ease
      Of tranquil happy mind,

And searched the garden's little length
    A fresh pleasaunce to find;
And there some yellow daffodils and jasmine hanging high
    Did rest the tired eye.

    The fairest and most fragrant
    Of the many sweets we found,
Was a little bush of daphne flower
    Upon a grassy mound,
And so thick were the blossoms set and so divine the scent
    That we were well content.

    Hungry for spring, I bent my head,
    The perfume fanned my face,
And all my soul was dancing
    In that lovely little place,
Dancing with a measured step from wrecked and shattered towns
    Away upon the Downs.

    I saw green banks of daffodil,
    Slim poplars in the breeze,
Great tan-brown hares in gusty March
    A-courting on the leas;
And meadows with their glittering streams, and silver scurrying
    dace,
    Home—what a perfect place!

                        E. WYNDHAM TENNANT. 1897–1916

Lament

    We who are left, how shall we look again
        Happily on the sun or feel the rain
    Without remembering how they who went
    Ungrudgingly and spent
    Their lives for us loved, too, the sun and rain?

    A bird among the rain-wet lilac sings—
    But we, how shall we turn to little things

And listen to the birds and winds and streams
Made holy by their dreams,
Nor feel the heart-break in the heart of things.

WILFRED WILSON GIBSON

The Soldier

If I should die, think only this of me:
    That there's some corner of a foreign field
That is for ever England. There shall be
    In that rich earth a richer dust concealed;
A dust whom England bore, shaped, made aware,
    Gave, once, her flowers to love, her ways to roam,
A body of England's, breathing English air,
    Washed by the rivers, blest by suns of home.

And think, this heart, all evil shed away,
    A pulse in the eternal mind, no less
        Gives somewhere back the thoughts by England
            given;
Her sights and sounds; dreams happy as her day;
    And laughter, learnt of friends; and gentleness,
        In hearts at peace, under an English heaven.

RUPERT BROOKE. 1887–1915

OLD FAVOURITES

A Christening Toast

To your mind—Peace,
To your heart—Joy,
To your soul—Strength
And Courage, Doy;*
In your outgoings
Nought amiss,
To your home-comings
Happiness.

DOROTHY UNA RATCLIFFE

The Song of the Shirt

With fingers weary and worn,
    With eyelids heavy and red
A woman sat, in unwomanly rags,
    Plying her needle and thread—
        Stitch! stitch! stitch!
In poverty, hunger, and dirt,
    And still with a voice of dolorous pitch
She sang the 'Song of the Shirt'.

'Work! work! work!
While the cock is crowing aloof!
    And work—work—work,
Till the stars shine through the roof!
It's oh! to be a slave
    Along with the barbarous Turk,
Where woman has never a soul to save,
    If this is Christian work!

'Work—work—work
Till the brain begins to swim;
    Work—work—work
Till the eyes are heavy and dim!
Seam, and gusset, and band,
    Band, and gusset, and seam,

* Dim. for darling

[265]

Till over the buttons I fall asleep,
    And sew them on in a dream!

'Oh, Men, with Sisters dear!
  Oh, Men, with Mothers and Wives!
It is not linen you're wearing out,
    But human creatures' lives!
        Stitch—stitch—stitch,
    In poverty, hunger, and dirt,
Sewing at once, with a double thread,
    A Shroud as well as a Shirt.

'But why do I talk of Death?
  That Phantom of grisly bone,
I hardly fear his terrible shape,
    It seems so like my own—
    It seems so like my own,
    Because of the fasts I keep;
O God! that bread should be so dear,
    And flesh and blood so cheap!

'Work—work—work!
  My labour never flags;
And what are its wages? a bed of straw,
    A crust of bread—and rags.
That shatter'd roof—and this naked floor—
    A table—a broken chair—
And a wall so blank, my shadow I thank
    For sometimes falling there!

'Work—work—work!
From weary chime to chime,
    Work—work—work—
As prisoners work for crime!
    Band, and gusset, and seam,
    Seam, and gusset, and band,
Till the heart is sick, and the brain benumb'd,
    As well as the weary hand.

'Work—work—work,
In the dull December light,
    And work—work—work,

When the weather is warm and bright—
While underneath the eaves
    The brooding swallows cling
As if to show me their sunny backs
    And twit me with the spring.

'Oh! but to breathe the breath
Of the cowslip and primrose sweet—
    With the sky above my head,
And the grass beneath my feet,
For only one short hour
    To feel as I used to feel,
Before I knew the woes of want
    And the walk that costs a meal!

'Oh! but for one short hour!
    A respite however brief!
No blessed leisure for Love or Hope,
    But only time for Grief!
A little weeping would ease my heart,
    But in their briny bed
My tears must stop, for every drop
    Hinders needle and thread!'

With fingers weary and worn,
    With eyelids heavy and red,
A woman sat in unwomanly rags,
    Plying her needle and thread—
        Stitch! stitch! stitch!
    In poverty, hunger, and dirt,
And still with a voice of dolorous pitch,—
Would that its tone could reach the Rich!—
    She sang this 'Song of the Shirt'.

THOMAS HOOD. 1799–1845

The Slave's Dream

Beside the ungathered rice he lay,
    His sickle in his hand;
His breast was bare, his matted hair

[267]

Was buried in the sand.
Again, in the mist and shadow of sleep,
    He saw his Native Land.

Wide through the landscape of his dreams
    The lordly Niger flowed;
Beneath the palm-trees on the plain
    Once more a king he strode;
And heard the tinkling caravans
    Descend the mountain-road.

He saw once more his dark-eyed queen
    Among her children stand;
They clasped his neck, they kissed his cheeks,
    They held him by the hand!—
A tear burst from the sleeper's lids
    And fell into the sand.

And then at furious speed he rode
    Along the Niger's bank;
His bridle-reins were golden chains,
    And, with a martial clank,
At each leap he could feel his scabbard of steel
    Smiting his stallion's flank.

Before him, like a blood-red flag,
    The bright flamingoes flew;
From morn till night he followed their flight,
    O'er plains where the tamarind grew,
    Till he saw the roofs of Caffre huts,
    And the ocean rose to view.

At night he heard the lion roar,
    And the hyæna scream,
And the river-horse, as he crushed the reeds
    Beside some hidden stream;
And it passed, like a glorious roll of drums,
    Through the triumph of his dream.

The forests, with their myriad tongues,
    Shouted of liberty;

And the Blast of the Desert cried aloud,
    With a voice so wild and free,
That he started in his sleep and smiled,
    At their tempestuous glee.

He did not feel the driver's whip,
    Nor the burning heat of day;
For Death had illumined the land of sleep,
    And his lifeless body lay
A worn-out fetter, that the soul
    Had broken and thrown away!

HENRY W. LONGFELLOW. 1807–1882

The Charge of the Light Brigade

I

Half a league, half a league,
    Half a league onward,
All in the valley of Death
    Rode the six hundred.
'Forward, the Light Brigade!
Charge for the guns!' he said:
Into the valley of Death
    Rode the six hundred.

II

'Forward the Light Brigade!'
Was there a man dismay'd?
Not tho' the soldier knew
    Some one had blunder'd:
Theirs not to make reply,
Theirs not to reason why,
Theirs but to do and die:
Into the valley of Death
    Rode the six hundred.

III

Cannon to right of them,
Cannon to left of them,

Cannon in front of them
    Volley'd and thunder'd;
Storm'd at with shot and shell,
Boldly they rode and well,
Into the jaws of Death,
Into the mouth of Hell
    Rode the six hundred.

IV

Flash'd all their sabres bare,
Flash'd as they turn'd in air,
Sabring the gunners there,
Charging an army, while
    All the world wonder'd:
Plunged in the battery-smoke
Right thro' the line they broke;
Cossack and Russian
Reel'd from the sabre-stroke
    Shatter'd and sunder'd.
Then they rode back, but not,
    Not the six hundred.

V

Cannon to right of them,
Cannon to left of them,
Cannon behind them
    Volley'd and thunder'd;
Storm'd at with shot and shell,
While horse and hero fell,
They that had fought so well
Came thro' the jaws of Death
Back from the mouth of Hell,
All that was left of them,
    Left of six hundred.

VI

When can their glory fade?
O the wild charge they made!
    All the world wonder'd.

Honour the charge they made!
Honour the Light Brigade,
    Noble six hundred.

ALFRED, LORD TENNYSON. 1809–1892

Lucy Gray: or Solitude

Oft I had heard of Lucy Gray:
And when I crossed the wild,
I chanced to see at break of day
The solitary child.

No mate, no comrade Lucy knew;
She dwelt on a wide moor—
The sweetest thing that ever grew
Beside a human door!

You yet may spy the fawn at play,
The hare upon the green;
But the sweet face of Lucy Gray
Will never more be seen.

'To-night will be a stormy night—
You to the town must go;
And take a lantern, child, to light
Your mother through the snow.'

'That, father, I will gladly do:
'Tis scarcely afternoon—
The minster-clock has just struck two,
And yonder is the moon.'

At this the father raised his hook,
And snapped a faggot band;
He plied his work;—and Lucy took
The lantern in her hand.

Not blither is the mountain roe:
With many a wanton stroke
Her feet disperse the powdery snow,
That rises up like smoke.

The storm came on before its time:
She wandered up and down;
And many a hill did Lucy climb;
But never reached the town.

The wretched parents all that night
Went shouting far and wide;
But there was neither sound nor sight
To serve them for a guide.

At daybreak on a hill they stood
That overlooked the moor;
And thence they saw the bridge of wood,
A furlong from their door.

They wept, and turning homeward, cried,
'In heaven we all shall meet:'
When in the snow the mother spied
The print of Lucy's feet.

Then downward from the steep hill's edge
They track the footmarks small;
And through the broken hawthorn hedge,
And by the long stone-wall;

And then an open field they crossed:
The marks were still the same;
They tracked them on, nor ever lost;
And to the bridge they came.

They followed from the snowy bank
Those footmarks, one by one,
Into the middle of the plank;
And further there were none!

Yet some maintain that to this day
She is a living child;
That you may see sweet Lucy Gray
Upon the lonesome wild.

O'er rough and smooth she trips along,
And never looks behind;
And sings a solitary song
That whistles in the wind.

WILLIAM WORDSWORTH. 1770–1850

Home-Thoughts from Abroad

O, to be in England
    Now that April's there,
And whoever wakes in England
Sees, some morning, unaware,
That the lowest boughs and the brushwood sheaf
Round the elm-tree bole are in tiny leaf,
While the chaffinch sings on the orchard bough
In England—now!

And after April, when May follows,
And the whitethroat builds, and all the swallows!
Hark, where my blossom'd pear-tree in the hedge
Leans to the field and scatters on the clover
Blossoms and dewdrops—at the bent spray's edge—
That's the wise thrush; he sings each song twice over,
Lest you should think he never could recapture
The first fine careless rapture!
And though the fields look rough with hoary dew,
All will be gay when noontide wakes anew
The buttercups, the little children's dower
—Far brighter than this gaudy melon-flower!

ROBERT BROWNING. 1812–1889

The Three Fishers

Three fishers went sailing away to the West,
    Away to the West as the sun went down;
Each thought on the woman who loved him the best,
    And the children stood watching them out of the town;

S
[273]

For men must work, and women must weep,
And there's little to earn, and many to keep,
    Though the harbour bar be moaning.

Three wives sat up in the lighthouse tower,
    And they trimmed the lamps as the sun went down;
They looked at the squall, and they looked at the shower,
    And the night-rack came rolling up ragged and brown.
    But men must work, and women must weep,
    Though storms be sudden, and waters deep,
        And the harbour bar be moaning.

Three corpses lay out on the shining sands
    In the morning gleam as the tide went down,
And the women are weeping and wringing their hands
    For those who will never come home to the town;
    For men must work, and women must weep,
    And the sooner it's over, the sooner to sleep;
        And good-bye to the bar and its moaning.

CHARLES KINGSLEY. 1819–1875

Paul Revere's Ride

Listen, my children, and you shall hear
Of the midnight ride of Paul Revere,
On the eighteenth of April, in seventy-five;
Hardly a man is now alive
Who remembers that famous day and year.

He said to his friend, 'If the British march
By land or sea from the town to-night,
Hang a lantern aloft in the belfry-arch
Of the North Church tower as a signal light,—
One if by land, and two if by sea;
And I on the opposite shore will be,
Ready to ride and spread the alarm
Through every Middlesex village and farm,
For the country-folk to be up and to arm.'

Then he said, 'Good-night!' and with muffled oar
Silently rowed to the Charlestown shore,
Just as the moon rose over the bay,
Where swinging wide at her moorings lay
The Somerset, British man-of-war;
A phantom-ship, with each mast and spar
Across the moon like a prison bar,
And a huge black hulk, that was magnified
By its own reflection in the tide.

Meanwhile, his friend through alley and street
Wanders and watches with eager ears,
Till in the silence around him he hears
The muster of men at the barrack-door,
The sound of arms, and the tramp of feet,
And the measured tread of the grenadiers,
Marching down to their boats on the shore.
Then he climbed to the tower on the Old North Church,
Up the wooden stairs, with stealthy tread,
To the belfry-chamber overhead,
And startled the pigeons from their perch
On the sombre rafters, that round him made
Masses and moving shapes of shade,—
Up the trembling ladder, steep and tall,
To the highest window in the wall,
Where he paused to listen and look down
A moment on the roofs of the town
And the moonlight flowing over all.

Beneath, in the churchyard, lay the dead,
In their night-encampment on the hill,
Wrapped in silence so deep and still
That he could hear, like a sentinel's tread,
The watchful night-wind, as it went
Creeping along from tent to tent,
And seeming to whisper, 'All is well!'
A moment only he feels the spell
Of the place and the hour, and the secret dread
Of the lonely belfry and the dead:
For suddenly all his thoughts are bent

On a shadowy something far away,
Where the river widens to meet the bay,—
A line of black that bends and floats
On the rising tide like a bridge of boats.

Meanwhile, impatient to mount and ride,
Booted and spurred, with a heavy stride
On the opposite shore walked Paul Revere.
Now he patted his horse's side,
Now gazed at the landscape far and near,
Then, impetuous, stamped the earth,
And turned and tightened his saddle-girth;
But mostly he watched with eager search
The belfry tower of the Old North Church,
As it rose above the graves on the hill,
Lonely and spectral and sombre and still,
And lo! as he looks, on the belfry's height
A glimmer, and then a gleam of light!
He springs to the saddle, the bridle he turns,
But lingers and gazes, till full on his sight
A second lamp in the belfry burns!

A hurry of hoofs in village street,
A shape in the moonlight, a bulk in the dark,
And beneath, from the pebbles, in passing, a spark
Struck out by a steed flying fearless and fleet;
That was all! And yet, through the gloom and the light,
The fate of a nation was riding that night;
And the spark struck out by that steed in its flight
Kindled the land into flame with its heat.
He has left the village and mounted the steep,
And beneath him, tranquil and broad and deep,
Is the Mystic, meeting the ocean tides;
And under the alders that skirt its edge,
Now soft on the sand, now loud on the ledge,
Is heard the tramp of his steed as he rides.

It was twelve by the village clock
When he crossed the bridge into Midford town.
He heard the crowing of the cock

And the barking of the farmer's dog,
And felt the damp of the river fog,
That rises after the sun goes down.
It was one by the village clock
When he galloped into Lexington.
He saw the gilded weather-cock.
Swim in the moonlight as he passed,
And the meeting-house windows blank and bare,
Gaze at him with a spectral glare,
As if they already stood aghast
At the bloody work they would look upon.

It was two by the village clock,
When he came to the bridge in Concord town.
He heard the bleating of the flock,
And the twitter of birds among the trees,
And felt the breath of the morning breeze
Blowing over the meadows brown.
And one was safe and asleep in his bed
Who at the bridge would be first to fall,
Who that day would be lying dead,
Pierced by a British musket-ball.

You know the rest. In the books you have read,
How the British regulars fired and fled,—
How the farmers gave them ball for ball,
From behind each fence and farmyard wall,
Chasing the red-coats down the lane,
Then crossing the fields to emerge again
Under the trees at the turn of the road,
And only pausing to fire and load.
So through the night rode Paul Revere;
And so through the night went his cry of alarm
To every Middlesex village and farm,—
A cry of defiance and not of fear,
A voice in the darkness, a knock at the door,
And a word that shall echo for evermore.
For, borne on the night-wind of the Past!
Through all our history, to the last,
In the hour of darkness and peril and need,

The people will waken and listen to hear
The hurrying hoof-beats of that steed,
And the midnight message of Paul Revere.

HENRY W. LONGFELLOW. 1807–1892

About Ben Adham and the Angel

Abou Ben Adham (may his tribe increase)
Awoke one night from a deep dream of peace,
And saw, within the moonlight in his room,
Making it rich, and like a lily in bloom,
An angel, writing in a book of gold:—
Exceeding peace had made Ben Adham bold,
And to the presence in the room he said,
'What writest thou?'—The vision raised its head,
And, with a look made of all sweet accord,
Answered, 'The names of those who love the Lord.'
'And is mine one?' said Abou. 'Nay, not so,'
Replied the angel. Abou spoke more low,
But cheerily still; and said, 'I pray thee, then,
Write me as one that loves his fellow-men.'

The angel wrote, and vanished. The next night
It came again with a great wakening light,
And showed the names whom love of God had blessed,
And lo! Ben Adhem's name led all the rest.

LEIGH HUNT. 1784–1859

The Brook

I come from haunts of coot and hern,
    I make a sudden sally
And sparkle out among the fern,
    To bicker down a valley.

By thirty hills I hurry down,
    Or slip between the ridges,
By twenty thorps, a little town,
    And half a hundred bridges.

Till last by Phillip's farm I flow
 To join the brimming river,
For men may come and men may go,
 But I go on for ever.

I chatter over stony ways,
 In little sharps and trebles,
I bubble into eddying bays,
 I babble on the pebbles.

With many a curve my banks I fret
 By many a field and fallow,
And many a fairy foreland set
 And willow-weed and mallow.

I chatter, chatter, as I flow
 To join the brimming river,
For men may come and men may go,
 But I go on for ever.

I wind about, and in and out,
 With here a blossom sailing,
And here and there a lusty trout,
 And here and there a grayling,

And here and there a foamy flake
 Upon me, as I travel
With many a silvery waterbreak
 Above the golden gravel,

And draw them all along, and flow
 To join the brimming river,
For men may come and men may go,
 But I go on for ever.

I steal by lawns and grassy plots
 I slide by hazel covers;
I move the sweet forget-me-nots
 That grow for happy lovers.

I slip, I slide, I gloom, I glance
    Among my skimming swallows;
I make the netted sunbeam dance
    Against my sandy shallows.

I murmur under moon and stars
    In brambly wildernesses;
I linger by my shingly bars;
    I loiter round my cresses;

And out again I curve and flow
    To join the brimming river,
For men may come and men may go,
    But I go on for ever.

                    ALFRED, LORD TENNYSON. 1809–1892

Past and Present

I remember, I remember
The house where I was born,
The little window where the sun
Came peeping in at morn;
He never came a wink too soon,
Nor brought too long a day,
But now I often wish the night
Had borne my breath away.

I remember, I remember
The roses red and white,
The violets, and the lily-cups,
Those flowers made of light!
The lilac where the robin built,
And where my brother set
The laburnum on his birthday—
The tree is living yet!

I remember, I remember
Where I used to swing,
And thought the air must rush as fresh
To swallows on the wing;

My spirit flew in feathers then,
That is so heavy now,
And summer pools could hardly cool
The fever on my brow!

I remember, I remember
The fir-trees dark and high;
I used to think their slender tops
Were close against the sky:
It was a childish ignorance,
But now 'tis little joy
To know I'm farther off from heav'n
Than when I was a boy.

THOMAS HOOD. 1799–1845

To Daffodils

Fair daffodils, we weep to see
    You haste away so soon;
As yet the early-rising sun
    Has not attain'd his noon.
        Stay, stay

    Until the hasting day
        Has run
    But to the evensong;
And, having pray'd together, we
    Will go with you along.

We have short time to stay, as you,
    We have as short a spring;
As quick a growth to meet decay,
    As you, or anything.
        We die
    As your hours do, and dry
        Away
    Like to the summer's rain;
Or as the pearls of morning's dew,
    Ne'er to be found again.

ROBERT HERRICK. 1591–1674

[281]

The Burial of Sir John Moore

Not a drum was heard, not a funeral note,
As his corpse to the rampart we hurried;
Not a soldier discharged his farewell shot
O'er the grave where our hero we buried.

We buried him darkly, at dead of night,
The sods with our bayonets turning,
By the struggling moonbeam's misty light,
And the lantern dimly burning.

No useless coffin enclosed his breast,
Nor in sheet nor in shroud we wound him;
But he lay like a warrior taking his rest,
With his martial cloak around him.

Few and short were the prayers we said,
And we spoke not a word of sorrow;
And we steadfastly gazed on the face of the dead,
And we bitterly thought of the morrow.

We thought, as we hollow'd his narrow bed,
And smooth'd down his lonely pillow,
That the foe and the stranger would tread o'er his head
And we far away on the billow!

Lightly they'll talk of the spirit that's gone,
And o'er his cold ashes upbraid him;—
But little he'll reck, if they let him sleep on
In the grave where a Briton has laid him.

But half of our heavy task was done,
When the clock struck the hour for retiring;
And we heard the distant and random gun
Of the enemy sullenly firing.

Slowly and sadly we laid him down,
From the field of his fame fresh and gory;
We carved not a line, and we raised not a stone—
But we left him alone with his glory!

Beth Gelert

The spearman heard the bugle sound, and cheerly smiled the
    morn,
And many a brach, and many a hound, attend Llewellyn's horn:
And still he blew a louder blast, and gave a louder cheer;
'Come, Gelert! why art thou the last Llewellyn's horn to hear?
Oh, where does faithful Gelert roam? the flower of all his race!
So true, so brave! a lamb at home—a lion in the chase!'

'Twas only at Llewellyn's board the faithful Gelert fed;
He watched, he served, he cheered his lord, and sentinel'd his bed.
In sooth, he was a peerless hound, the gift of royal John;—
But now no Gelert could be found, and all the chase rode on.

And now, as over rocks and dells the gallant chidings rise,
All Snowdon's craggy chaos yells with many mingled cries.
That day Llewellyn little loved the chase of hart or hare,
And scant and small the booty proved—for Gelert was not there.
Unpleased, Llewellyn homeward hied; when, near the portal seat,
His truant Gelert he espied, bounding his lord to greet.
But when he gained the castle door, aghast the chieftain stood;
The hound was smeared with gouts of gore:—his lips and fangs
    ran blood!
Llewellyn gazed with wild surprise, unused such looks to meet;
His favourite checked his joyful guise, and crouched, and licked
    his feet.

Onward in haste Llewellyn passed—and on went Gelert too;
And still, where'er his eyes were cast, fresh blood-gouts shocked
    his view!
O'erturned his infant's bed he found! the blood-stained covert
    rent;
And all around the walls and ground with recent blood besprent!
He called his child—no voice replied! he searched with terror
    wild:
Blood! blood! he found on every side, but nowhere found the
    child!

[283]

'Hell-hound! by thee my child's devoured!' the frantic father
      cried,
And to the hilt his vengeful sword he plunged in Gelert's side!—
His suppliant as to earth he fell, no pity could impart;
But still his Gelert's dying yell passed heavy o'er his heart.

Aroused by Gelert's dying yell, some slumberer wakened nigh—
What words the parent's joy can tell, to hear his infant cry!
Concealed beneath a mangled heap his hurried search had missed,
All glowing from his rosy sleep his cherub boy he kissed!
Nor scratch had he, nor harm, nor dread—But, the same couch
      beneath,
Lay a great wolf, all torn and dead—tremendous still in death!

Ah! what was then Llewellyn's pain! for now the truth was clear;
The gallant hound the wolf had slain, to save Llewellyn's heir.
Vain, vain was all Llewellyn's woe: 'Best of thy kind, adieu!
The frantic deed which laid thee low, this heart shall ever rue!'
—And now a gallant tomb they raise, with costly sculpture
      decked;
And marbles, storied with his praise, poor Gelert's bones protect.
Here never could the spearman pass, or forester, unmoved;
Here oft the tear-besprinkled grass Llewellyn's sorrow proved.
And here he hung his horn and spear; and oft, as evening fell,
In fancy's piercing sounds would hear poor Gelert's dying yell!

W. L. SPENCER

Break, Break, Break

Break, break, break,
      On thy cold grey stones, O Sea!
And I would that my tongue could utter
      The thoughts that arise in me.

O well for the fisherman's boy,
      That he shouts with his sister at play!
O well for the sailor lad,
      That he sings in his boat on the bay!

And the stately ships go on
    To their haven under the hill;
But O for the touch of a vanish'd hand,
    And the sound of a voice that is still!

Break, break, break,
    At the foot of thy crags, O Sea!
But the tender grace of a day that is dead
    Will never come back to me.

ALFRED, LORD TENNYSON. 1809–1892

The Vicar of Bray

In good King Charles's golden days,
    When Loyalty no harm meant;
A Furious High-Church Man I was,
    And so I gain'd Preferment.
Unto my Flock I daily Preach'd,
    Kings are by God appointed,
And Damn'd are those who dare resist,
    Or touch the Lord's Anointed.
        And this is Law, I will maintain
            Unto my Dying Day, Sir,
        That whatsoever King shall Reign,
            I will be Vicar of Bray, Sir!

When Royal James possest the Crown,
    And Popery grew in fashion;
The Penal Law I shouted down,
    And read the Declaration:
The Church of Rome, I found would fit,
    Full well my Constitution,
And I had been a Jesuit,
    But for the Revolution.
        And this is Law, etc.

When William our Deliverer came,
    To heal the Nation's Grievance,

I turned the Cat in Pan again,
    And swore to him Allegiance:
Old Principles I did revoke,
    Set Conscience at a distance,
Passive Obedience is a Joke,
    A Jest is Non-resistance.
        And this is Law, etc.

When glorious Anne became our Queen,
    The Church of England's Glory,
Another face of things was seen,
    And I became a Tory:
Occasional Conformists base,
    I Damn'd, and Moderation,
And thought the Church in danger was,
    From such Prevarication.
        And this is Law, etc.

When George in Pudding time came o'er,
    And Moderate Men looked big, Sir,
My Principles I chang'd once more,
    And so became a Whig, Sir:
And thus Preferment I procur'd,
    From our Faith's Great Defender,
And almost every day abjur'd
    The Pope, and the Pretender.
        And this is Law, etc.

The Illustrious House of Hannover,
    And Protestant Succession,
To these I lustily will swear,
    Whilst they can keep possession:
For in my Faith, and Loyalty,
    I never once will faulter,
But George, my Lawful King shall be,
    Except the Times shou'd alter.
        And this is Law, etc.

ANONYMOUS

Barbara Frietchie

Up from the meadows rich with corn,
Clear in the cool September morn,

The clustered spires of Frederick stand,
Green-walled by the hills of Maryland.

Round about them orchards sweep,
Apple and peach tree fruited deep,

Fair as the garden of the Lord
To the eyes of the famished rebel horde

On that pleasant morn of the early fall
When Lee marched over the mountain wall.

Over the mountains winding down,
Horse and foot into Frederick town,

Forty flags with their silver stars,
Forty flags with their crimson bars,

Flapped in the morning wind: the sun
Of noon looked down, and saw not one.

Up rose old Barbara Frietchie then,
Bowed with her fourscore years and ten;

Bravest of all in Frederick town,
She took up the flag the men hauled down;

In her attick window the staff she set,
To show that one heart was loyal yet.

Up the street came the rebel tread,
Stonewall Jackson riding ahead.

Under his slouched hat left and right
He glanced; the old flag met his sight.

'Halt!'—the dust-brown ranks stood fast.
'Fire!'—out blazed the rifle-blast.

It shivered the window, pane and sash;
It rent the banner with seam and gash.

Quick, as it fell, from the broken staff
Dame Barbara snatched the silken scarf.

She leaned far out on the window-sill,
And shook it forth with a royal will.

'Shoot, if you must, this old grey head,
But spare your country's flag,' she said.

A shade of sadness, a blush of shame,
Over the face of the leader came;

The nobler nature within him stirred
To life at that woman's deed and word:

'Who touches a hair of yon grey head
Dies like a dog! March on!' he said.

All day long through Frederick Street
Sounded the tread of marching feet:

All day long that free flag tost
Over the heads of the rebel host.

Ever its torn folds rose and fell
On the loyal winds that loved it well;

And through the hill-gaps sunset light
Shone over it with a warm good-night.

Barbara Frietchie's work is o'er,
And the rebel rides on his raids no more.

Honour to her! and let a tear
Fall, for her sake, on Stonewall's bier.

Over Barbara Frietchie's grave
Flag of Freedom and Union, wave!

Peace and order and beauty draw
Round thy symbol of light and law;

And ever the stars above look down
On thy stars below in Frederick town!

J. G. WHITTIER. 1807–1892

Lochinvar

O young Lochinvar is come out of the west,
Through all the wide border his steed was the best;
And save his good broadsword, he weapons had none,
He rode all unarmed, and he rode all alone.
So faithful in love, and so dauntless in war,
There never was knight like the young Lochinvar.

He staid not for brake, and he stopped not for stone,
He swam the Eske river where ford there was none;
But ere he alighted at Netherby gate,
The bride had consented, the gallant came late;
For a laggard in love, and a dastard in war,
Was to wed the fair Ellen of brave Lochinvar.

So boldly he entered the Netherby Hall,
Among bride's-men, and kinsmen, and brothers, and all:
Then spoke the bride's father, his hand on his sword,
(For the poor craven bridegroom said never a word),
'O come ye in peace here, or come ye in war,
Or to dance at our bridal, young Lord Lochinvar?'

'I long wooed your daughter, my suit you denied;—
Love swells like the Solway, but ebbs like its tide—
And now am I come, with this lost love of mine,
To lead but one measure, drink one cup of wine.
There are maidens in Scotland more lovely by far,
That would gladly be bride to the young Lochinvar.'

T [289]

The bride kissed the goblet: the knight took it up,
He quaffed off the wine, and he threw down the cup.
She looked down to blush, and she looked up to sigh,
With a smile on her lips, and a tear in her eye.
He took her soft hand, ere her mother could bar,—
'Now tread we a measure!' said young Lochinvar.

So stately his form, and so lovely her face,
That never a hall such a galliard did grace;
While her mother did fret, and her father did fume,
And the bridegroom stood dangling his bonnet and plume;
And the bride-maidens whispered, ''Twere better by far,
To have matched our fair cousin with young Lochinvar.'

One touch to her hand, and one word in her ear,
When they reached the hall-door, and the charger stood near;
So light to the croupe the fair lady he swung,
So light to the saddle before her he sprung!
'She is won! we are gone, over bank, bush, and scaur;
They'll have fleet steeds that follow,' quoth young Lochinvar.

There was mounting 'mong Graemes of the Netherby clan;
Forsters, Fenwicks, and Musgraves, they rode and they ran:
There was racing and chasing on Cannobie Lee,
But the lost bride of Netherby ne'er did they see.
So daring in love, and so dauntless in war,
Have ye e'er heard of gallant like young Lochinvar?

SIR WALTER SCOTT. 1771–1832

Daffodils

I wander'd lonely as a cloud
    That floats on high o'er vales and hills,
When all at once I saw a crowd,
    A host, of golden daffodils;
Beside the lake, beneath the trees,
Fluttering and dancing in the breeze.

Continuous as the stars that shine
    And twinkle on the Milky Way,
They stretch'd in never-ending line
    Along the margin of a bay:
Ten thousand saw I at a glance,
Tossing their heads in sprightly dance.

The waves beside them danced, but they
    Outdid the sparkling waves in glee:
A poet could not but be gay,
    In such a jocund company:
I gazed—and gazed—but little thought
What wealth the show to me had brought:

For oft, when on my couch I lie
    In vacant or in pensive mood,
They flash upon that inward eye
    Which is the bliss of solitude;
And then my heart with pleasure fills,
And dances with the daffodils.

WILLIAM WORDSWORTH. 1770–1850

The Lady of Shalott

PART I

On either side the river lie
Long fields of barley and of rye,
That clothe the wold and meet the sky;
And thro' the field the road runs by
        To many-tower'd Camelot;
And up and down the people go,
Gazing where the lilies blow
Round an island there below,
        The island of Shalott.

Willows whiten, aspens quiver,
Little breezes dusk and shiver
Thro' the wave that runs for ever

By the island in the river
        Flowing down to Camelot.
Four gray walls, and four gray towers,
Overlook a space of flowers,
And the silent isle embowers
        The Lady of Shalott.

By the margin, willow-veil'd,
Slide the heavy barges trail'd
By slow horses; and unhail'd
The shallop flitteth silken sail'd
        Skimming down to Camelot:
But who hath seen her wave her hand?
Or at the casement seen her stand?
Or is she known in all the land,
        The Lady of Shalott?

Only reapers, reaping early
In among the bearded barley,
Hear a song that echoes cheerly
From the river winding clearly,
        Down to tower'd Camelot:
And by the moon the reaper weary,
Piling sheaves in uplands airy,
Listening, whispers ''Tis the fairy
        Lady of Shalott.'

PART II

There she weaves by night and day
A magic web with colours gay.
She has heard a whisper say,
A curse is on her if she stay
        To look down to Camelot.
She knows not what the curse may be,
And so she weaveth steadily,
And little other care hath she,
        The Lady of Shalott.

And moving thro' a mirror clear
That hangs before her all the year,

Shadows of the world appear.
There she sees the highway near
       Winding down to Camelot:
There the river eddy whirls,
And there the surly village-churls,
And the red cloaks of market girls,
       Pass onward from Shalott.

Sometimes a troop of damsels glad,
An abbot on an ambling pad,
Sometimes a curly shepherd-lad,
Or long-hair'd page in crimson clad,
       Goes by to tower'd Camelot;
And sometimes thro' the mirror blue
The knights come riding two and two:
She hath no loyal knight and true,
       The Lady of Shalott.

But in her web she still delights
To weave the mirror's magic sights,
For often thro' the silent nights
A funeral, with plumes and lights,
       And music, went to Camelot:
Or when the moon was overhead,
Came two young lovers lately wed;
'I am half sick of shadows,' said
       The Lady of Shalott.

PART III

A bow-shot from her bower-eaves,
He rode between the barley-sheaves,
The sun came dazzling thro' the leaves,
And flamed upon the brazen greaves
       Of bold Sir Lancelot.
A red-cross knight for ever kneel'd
To a lady in his shield,
That sparkled on the yellow field
       Beside remote Shalott.

[293]

The gemmy bridle glitter'd free,
Like to some branch of stars we see
Hung in the golden Galaxy.
The bridle bells rang merrily
        As he rode down to Camelot;
And from his blazen'd baldric slung
A mighty silver bugle hung,
And as he rode his armour rung,
        Beside remote Shalott.

All in the blue unclouded weather
Thick-jewell'd shone the saddle-leather,
The helmet and the helmet-feather
Burn'd like one burning flame together,
        As he rode down to Camelot.
As often thro' the purple night,
Below the starry clusters bright,
Some bearded meteor, trailing light,
        Moves over still Shalott.

His broad clear brow in sunlight glow'd;
On burnish'd hooves his war-horse trode;
From underneath his helmet flow'd
His coal black curls as on he rode,
        As he rode down to Camelot.
From the bank and from the river
He flash'd into the crystal mirror,
'Tirra lirra,' by the river
        Sang Sir Lancelot.

She left the web, she left the loom,
She made three paces thro' the room,
She saw the water-lily bloom,
She saw the helmet and the plume,
        She look'd down to Camelot.
Out flew the web and floated wide;
The mirror crack'd from side to side;
'The curse is come upon me,' cried
        The Lady of Shalott.

PART IV

In the stormy east-wind straining,
The pale yellow woods were waning,
The broad stream in his banks complaining,
Heavily the low sky raining
   Over tower'd Camelot;
Down she came and found a boat
Beneath a willow left afloat,
And round about the prow she wrote
   The Lady of Shalott.

And down the river's dim expanse—
Like some bold seer in a trance,
Seeing all his own mischance—
With a glassy countenance
   Did she look to Camelot.
And at the closing of the day
She loosed the chain, and down she lay;
The broad stream bore her far away,
   The Lady of Shalott.

Lying robed in snowy white
That loosely flew to left and right—
The leaves upon her falling light—
Thro' the noises of the night
   She floated down to Camelot:
And as the boat-head wound along
The willowy hills and fields among,
They heard her singing her last song,
   The Lady of Shalott.

Heard a carol, mournful, holy,
Chanted loudly, chanted lowly,
Till her blood was frozen slowly,
And her eyes were darken'd wholly,
   Turn'd to tower'd Camelot;
For ere she reach'd upon the tide
The first house by the water-side,
Singing in her song she died,
   The Lady of Shalott.

Under tower and balcony,
By garden-wall and gallery,
A gleaming shape she floated by,
Dead-pale between the houses high,
      Silent into Camelot.
Out upon the wharfs they came,
Knight and burgher, lord and dame,
And round the prow they read her name,
      The Lady of Shalott.

Who is this? and what is here?
And in the lighted palace near
Died the sound of royal cheer;
And they cross'd themselves for fear,
      All the knights at Camelot;
But Lancelot mused a little space;
He said, 'She has a lovely face;
God in his mercy lend her grace,
      The Lady of Shalott.'

ALFRED, LORD TENNYSON. 1809–1892

Elegy

Written in a Country Churchyard.

The curfew tolls the knell of parting day,
  The lowing herd winds slowly o'er the lea,
The ploughman homeward plods his weary way,
  And leaves the world to darkness and to me.

Now fades the glimmering landscape on the sight,
  And all the air a solemn stillness holds,
Save where the beetle wheels his droning flight,
  And drowsy tinklings lull the distant folds,

Save that from yonder ivy-mantled tower
  The moping owl does to the moon complain
Of such as, wandering near her secret bower,
  Molest her ancient solitary reign.

Beneath those rugged elms, that yew-tree's shade,
    Where heaves the turf in many a mouldering heap,
Each in his narrow cell for ever laid,
    The rude forefathers of the hamlet sleep

The breezy call of incence-breathing morn,
    The swallow twittering from the straw-built shed,
The cock's shrill clarion, or the echoing horn,
    No more shall rouse them from their lowly bed.

For them no more the blazing hearth shall burn,
    Or busy housewife ply her evening care:
No children run to lisp their sire's return,
    Or climb his knees the envied kiss to share.

Oft did the harvest to their sickle yield,
    Their furrow oft the stubborn glebe has broke;
How jocund did they drive their team afield!
    How bowed the woods beneath their sturdy stroke.

Let not Ambition mock their useful toil,
    Their homely joys, and destiny obscure;
Nor Grandeur hear with a disdainful smile
    The short and simple annals of the Poor.

The boast of heraldry, the pomp of power,
    And all that beauty, all that wealth e'er gave
Await alike th'inevitable hour—
    The paths of glory lead but to the grave.

Nor you, ye Proud, impute to these the fault
    If Memory o'er their tomb no trophies raise,
Where, through the long-drawn aisle and fretted vault,
    The pealing anthem swells the note of praise.

Can storied urn or animated bust
    Back to its mansion call the fleeting breath?
Can Honour's voice provoke the silent dust,
    Or Flattery soothe the dull cold ear of Death?

U   [297]

Perhaps in this neglected spot is laid
    Some heart once pregnant with celestial fire;
Hands, that the rod of empire might have swayed,
    Or waked to ecstasy the living lyre:

But Knowledge to their eyes her ample page,
    Rich with the spoils of time, did ne'er unroll:
Chill Penury repressed their noble rage,
    And froze the genial current of the soul.

Full many a gem of purest ray serene
    The dark unfathomed caves of ocean bear;
Full many a flower is born to blush unseen,
    And waste its sweetness on the desert air.

Some village Hampden, that with dauntless breast
    The little tyrant of his fields withstood,
Some mute inglorious Milton here may rest,
    Some Cromwell, guiltless of his country's blood.

The applause of listening senates to command,
    The threats of pain and ruin to despise,
To scatter plenty o'er a smiling land,
    And read their history in a nation's eyes

Their lot forbade: nor circumscribed alone
    Their growing virtues, but their crimes confined;
Forbade to wade through slaughter to a throne,
    And shut the gates of mercy on mankind;

The struggling pangs of conscious truth to hide,
    To quench the blushes of ingenuous shame,
Or heap the shrine of Luxury and Pride
    With incense kindled at the Muse's flame.

Far from the madding crowd's ignoble strife
    Their sober wishes never learned to stray;
Along the cool sequestered vale of life
    They kept the noiseless tenour of their way.

Yet e'en these bones from insult to protect
    Some frail memorial still erected nigh,
With uncouth rhymes and shapeless sculpture decked,
    Implores the passing tribute of a sigh.

Their name, their years, spelt by the unlettered Muse,
    The place of fame and elegy supply;
And many a holy text around she strews
    That teach the rustic moralist to die.

For who, to dumb forgetfulness a prey,
    This pleasing anxious being e'er resigned,
Left the warm precincts of the cheerful day,
    Nor cast one longing lingering look behind?

On some fond breast the parting soul relies,
    Some pious drops the closing eye requires;
E'en from the tomb the voice of Nature cries,
    E'en in our ashes live their wonted fires.

For thee, who, mindful of th' unhonoured dead,
    Dost in these lines their artless tale relate;
If chance, by lonely Contemplation led,
    Some kindred spirit shall inquire thy fate,—

Haply some hoary-headed swain may say,
    Oft have we seen him at the peep of dawn
Brushing with hasty steps the dews away,
    To meet the sun upon the upland lawn;

There at the foot of yonder nodding beech,
    That wreathes its old fantastic roots so high,
His listless length at noon-tide would he stretch
    And pore upon the brook that babbles by.

Hard by yon wood, now smiling as in scorn,
    Muttering his wayward fancies he would rove,
Now drooping, woful-wan, like one forlorn,
    Or crazed with care or crossed in hopeless love.

One morn I missed him on the customed hill,
    Along the heath, and near his favourite tree;
Another came; nor yet beside the rill,
    Nor up the lawn, nor at the wood was he;

The next with dirges due in sad array
    Slow through the church-way path we saw him borne,
Approach and read (for thou canst read) the lay
    Graved on the stone beneath yon aged thorn.

THE EPITAPH

Here rests his head upon the lap of Earth
    A Youth, to Fortune and to Fame unknown;
Fair Science frowned not on his humble birth,
    And Melancholy marked him for her own.

Large was his bounty, and his soul sincere;
    Heaven did a recompense as largely send;
He gave to Misery all he had, a tear,
    He gained from Heaven, 'twas all he wished, a friend.

No further seek his merits to disclose,
    Or draw his frailties from their dread abode
(There they alike in trembling hope repose),
    The bosom of his Father and his God.

THOMAS GRAY. 1716–1771

Lord Ullin's Daughter

A Chieftain to the Highlands bound,
    Cries, 'Boatman, do not tarry;
And I'll give thee a silver pound
    To row us o'er the ferry.'

'Now who be ye would cross Loch Gyle,
    This dark and stormy water?'
'Oh! I'm the chief of Ulva's Isle,
    And this Lord Ullin's daughter.

[300]

'And fast before her father's men
    Three days we've fled together;
For should he find us in the glen,
    My blood would stain the heather.

'His horsemen hard behind us ride;
    Should they our steps discover,
Then who will cheer my bonny bride
    When they have slain her lover?'

Outspoke the hardy Highland wight:
    'I'll go, my chief—I'm ready;
It is not for your silver bright,
    But for your winsome lady.

'And by my word, the bonny bird
    In danger shall not tarry;
So, though the waves are raging white,
    I'll row you o'er the ferry.'

By this the storm grew loud apace,
    The water-wraith was shrieking;
And in the scowl of heaven each face
    Grew dark as they were speaking.

But still, as wilder blew the wind,
    And as the night grew drearer,
Adown the glen rode armed men—
    Their tramping sounded nearer.

'Oh! haste thee, haste!' the lady cries,
    'Though tempests round us gather;
I'll meet the raging of the skies,
    But not an angry father.'

The boat has left a stormy land,
    A stormy sea before her—
When oh! too strong for human hand,
    The tempest gathered o'er her.

[301]

And still they rowed amidst the roar
    Of waters fast prevailing;
Lord Ullin reach'd that fatal shore—
    His wrath was turned to wailing.

For sore dismay'd through storm and shade,
    His child he did discover;
One lovely arm she stretch'd for aid,
    And one was round her lover.

'Come back! come back!' he cried in grief,
    'Across this stormy water;
And I'll forgive your Highland chief,
    My daughter!—oh, my daughter!'

'Twas vain: the loud waves lash'd the shore,
    Return or aid preventing;
The waters wild went o'er his child,
    And he was left lamenting.

THOMAS CAMPBELL. 1777–1884

November in London

No sun—no moon—
No morn—no noon—
No dawn—no dusk—no proper time of day—
No sky—no earthly view—
No distance looking blue—
No road—no street—no 't'other side the way'—
No end to any row—
No indications where the crescents go—
No top to any steeple—
No recognitions of familiar people—
No courtesies for showing 'em—
No knowing 'em!
No travelling at all—no locomotion,
No inkling of the way—no notion—
'No go'—by land or ocean—
No mail—no post—

No news from any foreign coast—
No park—no ring—no afternoon gentility—
No company—no nobility—
No warmth, no cheerfulness, no healthful ease—
No comfortable feel in any member—
No shade, no shine, no butterflies, no bees—
No fruits, no flowers, no leaves, no trees—
November!

THOMAS HOOD. 1798–1845

The Vale of Avoca

There is not in the wide world a valley so sweet,
As that vale in whose bosom the bright waters meet,
Oh! the last rays of feeling and life must depart,
Ere the bloom of that valley shall fade from my heart.

Yet it was not that Nature had shed o'er the scene
Her purest of crystal and brightest of green;
'Twas not her soft magic of streamlet or hill,
Oh! no—it was something more exquisite still.

'Twas that friends, the beloved of my bosom were near,
Who made every dear scene of enchantment more dear.
And who felt how the best charms of Nature improve,
When we see them reflected from looks that we love.

Sweet vale of Avoca! how calm could I rest
In thy bosom of shade, with the friends I love best,
Where the storms that we feel in this cold world should cease,
And our hearts, like thy waters, be mingled in peace.

THOMAS MOORE. 1779–1852

The Inchcape Rock

No stir in the air, no stir in the sea,
The ship was still as she could be,
Her sails from heaven received no motion
Her keel was steady in the ocean.

[303]

Without either sign or sound of their shock
The waves flowed over the Inchcape Rock;
So little they rose, so little they fell,
They did not move the Inchcape Bell.

The worthy Abbot of Aberbrothok
Had placed that bell on the Inchcape Rock;
On a buoy in the storm it floated and swung,
And over the waves its warning rung.

When the rock was hid by the surges' swell,
The mariners heard the warning bell;
And then they knew the perilous rock,
And blest the Abbot of Aberbrothok.

The sun in heaven was shining gay,
All things were joyful on that day;
The sea-birds screamed as they wheel'd round,
And there was joyaunce in their sound.

The buoy of the Inchcape Bell was seen,
A darker speck on the ocean green;
Sir Ralph the Rover walk'd his deck,
And he fixed his eye on the darker speck.

He felt the cheering power of spring,
It made him whistle, it made him sing;
His heart was mirthful to excess,
But the Rover's mirth was wickedness.

His eye was on the Inchcape float;
Quoth he, 'My men, put out the boat,
And row me to the Inchcape Rock,
And I'll plague the Abbot of Aberbrothok.'

The boat is lower'd the boatsmen row,
And to the Inchcape Rock they go;
Sir Ralph bent over from the boat,
And he cut the bell from the Inchcape float.

Down sank the bell with a gurgling sound,
The bubbles rose and burst around:
Quoth Sir Ralph, 'The next who comes to the Rock
Won't bless the Abbot of Aberbrothok.'

Sir Ralph the Rover sail'd away,
He scour'd the seas for many a day;
And now, grown rich with plunder'd store,
He steers his course for Scotland's shore.

So thick a haze o'erspreads the sky,
They cannot see the sun on high;
The wind hath blown a gale all day,
At evening it hath died away.

On deck the Rover takes his stand,
So dark it is they see no land.
Quoth Sir Ralph, 'It will be lighter soon,
For there is the dawn of the rising moon.'

'Canst hear,' said one, 'the breakers' roar?
For methinks we should be near the shore.'
'Now where we are I cannot tell,
But I wish I could hear the Inchcape Bell!'

They hear no sound, the swell is strong;
Though the wind hath fallen they drift along,
Till the vessel strikes with a shivering shock,—
'Oh! heavens! it is the Inchcape Rock!'

Sir Ralph the Rover tore his hair,
He cursed himself in his despair;
The waves rush in on every side,
The ship is sinking beneath the tide.

But even now in his dying fear
One dreadful sound could the Rover hear,
A sound as if with the Inchcape Bell
The fiends in triumph were ringing his knell.

ROBERT SOUTHEY. 1774–1843

Envoy

Go, songs, for ended is our brief, sweet play;
     Go, children of swift joy and tardy sorrow:
And some are sung, and that was yesterday,
     And some unsung, and that may be to-morrow.

Go forth; and if it be o'er stony way,
     Old joy can lend what newer grief must borrow:
And it was sweet, and that was yesterday,
     And sweet is sweet, though purchased with sorrow.

Go, songs, and come not back from your far way:
     And if men ask you why ye smile and sorrow,
Tell them ye grieve, for your hearts know To-day,
     Tell them ye smile, for your eyes know To-morrow.

FRANCIS THOMPSON. 1859–1907

INDEX OF FIRST LINES

[309]